WOMEN WORKING

Current Books in Women's Studies

Basis of the Bargain: Gender, Schooling & Jobs Carol O'Donnell
Caring for Australia's Children: Political & Industrial Issues in Child Care Deborah Brennan & Carol O'Donnell
Contemporary Feminist Thought Hester Eisenstein
Crossing Boundaries: Feminisms & the Critique of Knowledges Edited by Barbara Caine E.A. Grosz & Marie de Lepervanche
Ethnicity, Class & Gender in Australia Edited by Gill Bottomley & Marie de Lepervanche
Female Crime: The Construction of Women in Criminology Ngaire Naffine
Feminist Challenges: Social & Political Theory Edited by Carole Pateman & Elizabeth Gross
Gender & Power R.W. Connell
Gender Agenda Terry Evans
Gender At Work Ann Game & Rosemary Pringle
Getting Equal: Labour Market Regulation and Women's Work Carol O'Donnell & Philippa Hall
Good & Mad Women: The Historical Construction of Femininity in Twentieth Century Australia Jill Julius Matthews
Program for Change Edited by Marian Sawer
Secretaries Talk: Sexuality, Power and Work Rosemary Pringle
Sexual Subversions: Three French Feminists Elizabeth Grosz
Short-changed: Women and Economic Policies Rhonda Sharp & Ray Broomhill
Staking a Claim: Feminism, Bureaucracy and the State Suzanne Franzway, Dianne Court and R.W. Connell
Subordination: Feminism & Social Theory Clare Burton
Teaching Gender? Sex Education & Sexual Stereotypes Tricia Szirom
Which Way Is Up? Essays on Class, Sex & Culture R.W. Connell
A Woman's Place: Women & Politics in Australia Marian Sawer & Marian Simms
Women, Social Science & Public Policy Edited by Jacqueline Goodnow & Carole Pateman

WOMEN WORKING

Economics and reality

Karen Mumford

Allen & Unwin
Sydney Wellington London Boston

First published in 1989
Allen & Unwin Australia Pty Ltd
An Unwin Hyman company
8 Napier Street, North Sydney, NSW 2059 Australia

Allen & Unwin New Zealand Limited
60 Cambridge Terrace, Wellington, New Zealand

Unwin Hyman Limited
15–17 Broadwick Street, London W1V 1FP England

Unwin Hyman Inc.
8 Winchester Place, Winchester, Mass 01890 USA

National Library of Australia
Cataloguing-in-Publication entry:

Mumford, Karen.
    Women working: economics and reality.

    Bibliography.
    Includes index.
    ISBN 0 04 332134 8.

    1. Women – Employment – Australia.
    2. Labor supply – Australia. I. Title.

331.4'0994

Library of Congress Catalog Card Number: 88–71988

Set in 10.5/12pt Aster by Graphicraft Typesetters, Hong Kong
Printed in Malaysia by SRM Production Services Sdn Bhd

Contents

vi *Women working*

Tables

Figures

Acknowledgements

The author owes thanks to too many people to list them all here. However, special thanks should go to David Matthews, Roger Tuckwell and Gus Hooke. Responsibility for any errors is, of course, my own.

I

Describing the labour market

1

Introduction

*There is no consensus concerning the causes of the rise
and persistence of sexual segregation in the labour force.
Furthermore, no attempt has been made to systematically
test the competing explanations.*

Donald E. Lewis, September 1982[1]

Women are second class workers in Australia. This book
does not attempt to cover all facets of females in the Australian workforce. Rather, the many theories used to explain,
justify or deny the labour market position of women are
concentrated on. This book looks at the way women's contribution to the workforce has been described and explained
by these theories and compares these descriptions and explanations with the available data.

The book is in two parts. The first provides a description
of the position of women in the Australian labour market
against which the various theories presented in the second
half will be evaluated. In Chapters 2–7 it is demonstrated
that women possess the educational levels required for
levels of occupations higher than those they actually fill;
that the occupations women work in have shown little
change since 1911, although the number of women in the
work force has increased greatly since the Second World
War; that women have only marginally higher rates of
absenteeism than males; that female trade unionism is
higher in male-dominated occupations than in female-
dominated ones; that the average female wage is some 30
per cent lower than the average wage of males. These are
some of the facts which provide the empirical features
which any adequate theory of the labour market should
be able to explain. For convenience of discussion, these

3

theories are aggregated according to their economic-political features in Chapters 8, 9 and 10 in the second part of the book.

Chapter 8 discusses the Orthodox theories: the Human Capital, Taste for Discrimination, Job Search, and Employer Screening theories. These theories contend that women lack the general education levels required by employers, that women don't stay in the work force long enough to warrant the expense of this education and even that women are more efficient at household duties than paid work force occupations.

Chapter 9 discusses Institutionalist theories: the Intra-Firm Segmentation, Market Efficiency, Monopsonistic Competition, and Over-crowding theories. These argue that women as a group are not as highly trained as men, that women have high absenteeism as well as high turnover, or that employers may be exploiting women by over-crowding them into small occupations which have high levels of competition.

Chapter 10 presents Radical theories: the Segmented Labour Markets, Neo-Marxist, and Feminist Power theories. According to these approaches women are exploited by the capitalist system; technology makes women redundant in the house and forces them out into poorly paid occupations. The Radical Feminist Power theory argues that capitalists use male workers to force women into under-paid positions and that women lack the trade union power they need to compete against this pressure.

Australia's Anti-Discrimination legislation and Affirmative Action policies are explained and discussed in Chapter 11. This chapter considers the usefulness of these government initiatives given the findings of the earlier chapters.

The book concludes with a discussion of the theories, their predictions, and the relevance of these to the results of earlier chapters and to an understanding of the Australian labour market.

2

Participation

Participating in a labour market does not just mean that a person is currently employed; all those people who want to work and are unable to find paid employment are also considered to be participants in the labour market. We can devise a 'participation rate' to compare groups in the labour market. The *participation rate* is equal to the labour force divided by the potential working population. The *labour force* is all those members of a group that want to work, or are already employed, in the labour market. The labour force can be calculated for workers as a whole, or for any category of workers such as women, or married women. Similarly, the *potential working population* can be estimated for the economy as a whole or for any subset of the economy such as women, or married women.

When calculating participation figures from their surveys, the Australian Bureau of Statistics (ABS) asks respondents if they have been actively seeking work in the fortnight prior to the survey. Of those out of work, only those respondents who answer this question positively are considered to have been participating in the labour market. One of the problems with this survey approach is that many workers who want to work may not be included in the ABS participation figures. This is because they become discouraged from actively seeking paid work and thus answer the survey question negatively. In Australia, in order to qualify for unemployment benefits from the Federal Government, recipients must prove that they have been actively seeking work. Women who cannot find work and become discouraged may return to performing household tasks without considering themselves as unemployed. Such women may not register

Table 2.1   Women in the Australian labour force, 1947–87

Year	Women proportion of the labour force (%)		Married women as a proportion of female labour force (%)	Women's labour force participation rate (%)	
	Married women	All women		Married women	All women
June 1947	3.4	22.4	15.3	6.5	24.9
June 1954	7.0	22.8	30.5	12.6	26.3
June 1961	9.6	25.1	38.3	17.3	28.9
June 1966	14.1	29.5	47.8	26.6	35.2
June 1971	18.0	31.7	56.8	32.8	37.1
June 1981	21.7	37.6	57.6	44.3	45.6
June 1983	21.1	37.5	57.4	44.0	44.4
June 1986	23.4	39.6	59.0	47.8	48.2
May 1987	23.7	40.1	59.0	49.2	49.1

Source: Eccles (1982), ABS (6203, 1984 and 1987)

with the Commonwealth Employment Service (CES) and actively seek work via their offices. The following data, which derives from the ABS surveys, should therefore be approached with caution. Typically the figures will underestimate the number of women who actually want to work and thus underestimate the true participation rates of women. Nevertheless, we can still glean some very interesting trends from the tables.

Changes in women's participation in the labour market since 1945

Australian women have greatly increased their participation in the labour force since the Second World War.[1] As Table 2.1[2] illustrates, although in 1947 only 24.9 per cent of women participated in the labour market, by 1987 this had risen to 49.1 per cent of all women over fifteen years. Women thus now make up a much larger proportion of the country's total labour force; rising from a proportion of 22.4 per cent in 1947 to 40.1 per cent of the total labour force in 1987. Nowadays, as a rough measure, one out of every two women is in the workforce, and two out of every five workers are female. Some authorities[3] predict that female participation rates will rise to 55.6 per cent by the year 2001.[4]

Table 2.1 also separates out married women, which helps to indicate that the major source for the rise in the female participation rate has been the rapid inflow of married women into the labour market, particularly during the sixties. In 1947 only 6.5 per cent of married women participated in the work force (or 3.4 per cent of the total labour force). By 1966 the figure had quadrupled to 26.6 per cent of married women working in the labour market (representing 14.1 per cent of the total workforce). Although the growth in participation rates subsequently slowed, they nevertheless continued to increase. The labour force participation of married women almost doubled between 1966 and 1987 when 49.2 per cent of married women worked in the labour market, almost equalling the participation rate of 49.1 per cent for all women. In 1987, married women made up 59.0 per cent of the female labour force and 23.7 per cent of the total labour force, a very substantial increase in their participation rates.

Figure 2.1[5] clearly shows the increase in labour force participation of married women relative to all women between 1947 and 1987: the lower line depicts the percentage of married women who are participating in the labour market, the higher line depicts all women (married and single combined). The gap between the two lines has fallen away quite dramatically in the last 40 years. In 1987 the proportion of married women working is virtually the same as the proportion of all women working. This rapid increase in the number of married women working represents a significant change in the attitudes of our society.

Age and women's participation

Figure 2.2[6] shows the participation profiles of women of different age groups in 1966, 1976 and 1987. Closer inspection reveals that the participation rates for women of all ages increased during this twenty-one year period, with the exception of juniors (15–19 years old) which showed some decrease. It is also evident that there have been relatively larger increases in female participation rates among the

Figure 2.1   Women's labour force participation, 1947–87

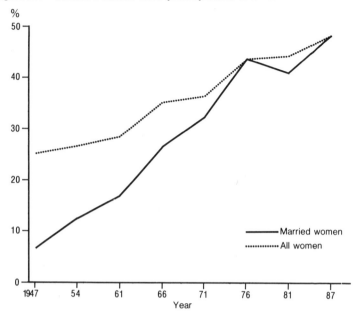

Source: Eccles (1982), ABS (6203, May 1987)

20–25 year and the 35 and over age brackets, especially among married women.

In the 1966–76 period, married women significantly increased their labour force participation rates, especially in the 30–34 year and 35–45 year age groups which rose by 2.1 and 2.3 percentage points respectively. This suggests that greater numbers of women are returning to the labour market after their childbearing years. Between 1976 and 1987, the participation rate for single women increased a little more rapidly than that of married women, but both showed similar trends with increases in the 25–29 year age group and constancy for the 35–44 year group.

A strong drop occurs in all the curves for the 25–35 year age group, but the extent of these falls in participation rates have decreased.[7] In the 1960s one-third of the female work force left the labour market during their prime childbearing years, by the 1980s this figure had decreased to approximately one-fifth of the female work force.

Thus, all adult women have increased their participation

Figure 2.2 Age participation profiles of women, 1966, 1976 and 1987

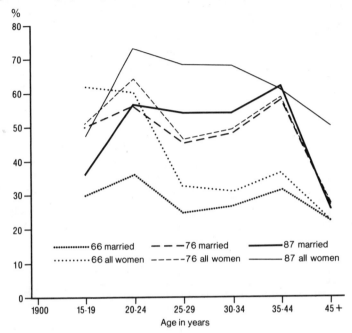

%

Legend:
·············· 66 married   — — —76 married   ●——— 87 married
··········· 66 all women   — — — 76 all women   ——— 87 all women

Age in years

Source: Eccles (1982), ABS (6203, 1987)

rates between 1966 and 1987, with especially strong surges in the participation rates of married women and of all women aged 30–45 years in the 1966 to 1976 time period. Women have also consistently decreased their tendency to leave the labour force in the 25–35 year age bracket over the period considered.

Full-time or part-time work

Figure 2.3[8] illustrates changes in the full-time and part-time participation rates of men and women between 1972 and 1987. Full-time participation rates for men fell by 9.5 percentage points[9] over this period but the full-time participation rates for women remained constant at around 30 per cent, while married women showed a slight *drop* of 1.2 percentage points in their full-time participation rates between 1972 and 1987.

Figure 2.3   Full-time, part-time participation, 1972–87

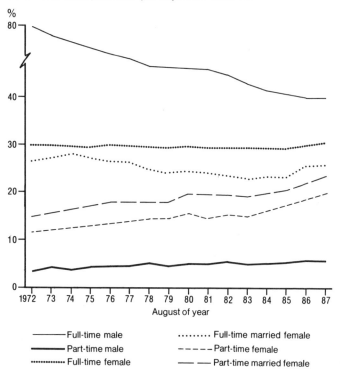

Source: ABS (6101, 1983 and 1986), ABS (6203, 1987)

Male *part-time* participation rates increased throughout the fifteen years by 1.9 percentage points.[10] Married women also increased their part-time participation rates between 1972 and 1987, but by a much larger amount than the men: the part-time participation rate for married women rose 8.6 percentage points during this period.[11] The participation rates for single women also rose 7.7 percentage points during this period.[12] Thus, both men and women increased their part-time participation rates between 1972 and 1987 though this trend was stronger for women than for men. The increase in the part-time participation rate of women was three times larger than the increase in the male part-time participation rate. And the gain in the part-time participation rate of married women was three and a half times larger than the increase in the male part-time participation rate.

The third major type of employment available in the labour market, apart from full-time and part-time employment, is casual employment. Working conditions for casual employees are typically inferior to those of either part or full-time workers: casual employees receive less notice of the hours they are expected to work and have no job security. Intuitively, there seems to be a link between increases in part-time participation rates and a rise in casual employment and, although there has been very little work undertaken on casual employment in Australia, a recent study by Dawkins and Norris[13] finds that there has been an increase in casual employment. This study suggests that many of these jobs have been taken by married women and young people, often because they cannot find preferred work. Casual employment typically occurs in lowly-skilled occupations where job security is poor and opportunity for promotion is rare.[14] The issue of increasing female participation rates in casual employment is a subject of concern, however more work is required in this area before strong conclusions can be reached.

To sum up, during the fifteen years from 1972 to 1987, women increased both their full-time and part-time *participation rates* relative to the male participation rates. This does not necessarily imply that women's full-time and part-time *employment rates* increased relative to male employment rates. Increasing participation rates may merely reflect an increase in the number of women seeking work. Many of these women who want work may not gain employment.[15]

Industrial and occupational employment

It is worthwhile to distinguish between the occupation and the industry that a worker finds employment in. The *occupation* of a worker refers to the nature of the tasks that that worker typically carries out. For instance, a nurse is skilled in caring for the sick, an accountant in maintaining financial records, and a chauffeur in driving cars. The *industry* that a worker is employed in is defined by the nature of the final product that workers produce. Thus, if the nurse, accountant and chauffeur all worked for a company whose primary aim was to produce steel then these workers would be in the steel industry.

Tables 2.2 and 2.3[16] consider the changes in *employment* of women and men in occupations and industries respectively over two periods, 1975–80 and 1980–85. Column one lists the total growth in the work force of that occupation in Table 2.2, or industry in Table 2.3, for each respective period. Column four lists the share of the change in this work force that is made up by women. Similarly, column five considers the share of the change in the occupation's or industry's work force that is made up by men. Column two considers the *rate* of change of employment for women within the occupation or industry. Similarly, column three considers the rate of change of employment for men within the occupation or industry. Columns six and seven list the final concentration rates of women and men employed for each of the occupations or industries. The total row at the base of each table sums the columns and provides us with growth rates for the economy as a whole.

Thus, in the 1975–80 period, the professional occupation increased its labour force by 31.1 per cent. Of this increase, 62.2 per cent were female and 37.8 per cent were male. This represented a 45.4 per cent increase in the number of women employed as professionals, and a 20.5 per cent increase in the number of men employed as professionals. The larger growth of the female work force, relative to the male work force, in the professional occupation reflects some balancing of gender in the work place.

From the total row it can be seen that the economy's total work force grew by 7.5 per cent between 1975 and 1980 and by 5.8 per cent between 1980–85. Women made up 63.1 per cent of the new employees during 1975–80 and 70.9 per cent of the new employees in 1980–85. This increased the female share of the economy's total employment by 3.9 percentage points, from 34.6 per cent to 38.5 per cent, decreasing the male share of total employment from 65.4 per cent to 61.6 per cent and represented a substantial increase in female employment relative to male employment throughout the decade 1975–85. This conclusion is supported by Figure 2.4.[17]

Table 2.2 Trends in segmentation of the labour force by occupation, August 1975–80, 1980–85

Occupation	Growth in labour force — Total 75–80 %	80–85 %	Female 75–80 %	80–85 %	Male 75–80 %	80–85 %	Of growth proportion — Female 75–80 %	80–85 %	Male 75–80 %	80–85 %	Final concentration — Female 75 %	80 %	85 %	Male 75 %	80 %	85 %
Professional, technical etc.	31.1	14.8	45.4	10.1	20.5	19.0	62.2	32.1	37.8	67.8	42.6	47.2	45.3	57.5	52.8	54.7
Admin., exec., managerial	11.9	13.9	36.0	47.4	8.8	8.6	34.0	46.6	65.8	53.5	11.2	13.7	17.7	88.8	86.4	82.3
Clerical	4.3	14.1	7.5	19.1	−2.4	2.3	117.5	95.3	−17.5	4.7	68.3	70.4	73.4	31.7	29.6	26.6
Sales	15.0	7.0	16.8	6.6	13.2	6.1	58.4	50.3	41.8	50.0	52.3	53.1	52.9	47.7	47.0	47.2
Farmers, fishermen, timber getters etc.	4.0	2.4	31.0	12.1	−1.6	−0.3	133.1	108.5	−33.1	−8.5	16.9	21.3	23.4	83.1	78.7	76.6
Transport, & communication	−6.6	2.8	2.8	−10.1	−8.0	5.1	5.7[a]	−53.3	−105.7	153.3	13.6	14.9	13.1	86.4	85.1	87.0
Tradesmen, prod. process, labourers, miners	1.2	−3.6	−5.4	−2.8	2.2	−3.8	56.1[b]	−9.2[c]	156.1	−90.8[c]	12.7	11.9	12.0	87.34	88.1	88.0
Service, sport, & recreation	7.9	6.0	6.3	7.0	11.0	4.3	51.4	74.0	48.7	26.0	65.0	63.9	64.5	35.1	36.1	35.5
Total	7.5	5.8	13.8	11.3	4.2	2.7	63.1	70.9	36.9	29.1	34.6	36.6	38.5	65.4	63.4	61.6

Notes: [a] gender has increased while total people employed fallen
  [b] gender has decreased while total people have increased
  [c] gender has decreased as has total population (ie, proportion of the fall in the total)

Source: ABS (6101, 1986: 45)

Table 2.3 Trends in segmentation of the labour force by industry, August 1975–80, 1980–85

Industry	LF growth: Total 75–80	Total 80–85	Female 75–80	Female 80–85	Male 75–80	Male 80–85	Growth prop: Female 75–80	Female 80–85	Male 75–80	Male 80–85	Final conc: Female 1975	Female 1980	Female 1985	Male 1975	Male 1980	Male 1985
Agriculture, forestry, fishing, hunting	2.4	1.7	24.9	15.3	-2.9	-2.5	196.9	213.0	-96.9[b]	112.0[b]	19.3	23.5	26.7	80.7	76.5	73.3
Mining	6.3	21.8	14.8	35.7	5.6	20.5	18.0	13.7	82.0	86.3	7.7	8.3	9.3	92.3	91.7	90.7
Manufacturing	-1.8	-10.5	-8.3	-0.7	0.5	-13.7	120.1[c]	1.7[c]	20.1[a]	98.3[c]	26.1	24.4	27.1	73.9	75.6	72.9
Electrical, gas, water	22.1	7.0	-12.5	23.1	25.8	5.8	-5.6[b]	23.3	105.6	76.7	9.9	7.1	8.1	90.1	92.9	91.9
Construction	-5.0	-3.4	68.6	19.8	-9.4	-6.1	77.9[a]	56.5[a]	-178.0[c]	-156.5[c]	5.6	10.0	12.4	94.4	90.1	87.6
Wholesale, retail	10.2	3.5	13.6	3.4	7.7	3.5	56.0	42.5	44.0	57.5	41.8	43.1	43.1	58.2	56.9	56.9
Transport, storage	3.8	9.4	14.5	12.1	2.1	8.9	52.4	19.6	47.6	80.4	13.8	15.2	15.6	86.2	84.8	84.4
Communication	-7.0	27.4	-1.6	2.9	-8.7	31.5	5.8[c]	15.7	93.1[c]	84.3	25.2	26.6	24.3	74.7	73.4	75.7
Finance, property, business services	19.6	28.9	16.4	34.5	22.4	24.4	38.0	53.0	62.0	46.9	45.6	44.3	46.3	54.4	55.5	53.7
Public Admin., Defence	1.7	14.6	1.4	26.3	2.0	8.6	27.1	61.3	75.0	38.7	34.2	34.1	37.6	65.7	65.9	62.4
Community services	27.9	13.9	33.0	12.8	19.8	15.7	72.3	59.2	27.3	40.8	61.6	64.0	63.4	38.5	36.0	36.6
Recreation, personal, other services	4.9	10.0	0.4	6.2	12.1	15.4	4.4	36.8	95.6	63.2	61.6	58.9	56.9	38.4	41.1	43.1
Total	7.5	5.8	13.8	11.3	4.3	2.7	63.1	70.9	36.9	29.1	34.6	36.6	38.5	65.4	63.4	61.5

Notes: [a] gender has increased while total people employed fallen
[b] gender has decreased while total people have increased
[c] gender has decreased as has total population (ie, proportion of the fall in the total)

Source: ABS (6101, 1986)

2.4 Aggregate hours worked, females/males, 1966–87

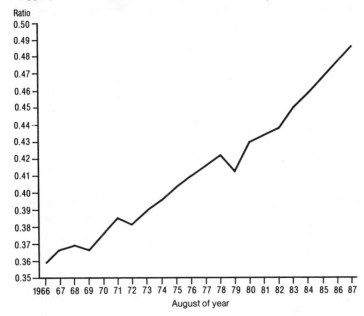

Source: Lewis (1983), ABS (6101, 1986) ABS (6203, 1987)

Figure 2.4 graphs the ratio of the aggregate hours worked by women to the aggregate hours worked by men from 1966 to 1987, that is, it compares the total hours worked (employment) of women divided by the total hours worked of men. For every 100 hours of work undertaken in Australia's labour market in 1966, women carried out 36 hours. By 1987 this ratio had risen to women carrying out some 48 per cent of all hours worked in the economy. Thus, the declines of 1969, 1972 and 1978 were more than compensated for by gains in the remainder of the 21-year-period.

Table 2.2 also provides details of the occupations in which women increased their employment numbers. From 1975–85 women increased their employment numbers relative to men in all but three occupations: transport and communication; tradesmen, production process workers, labourers, miners etc.; and service, sport and recreation (the last remaining strongly female-concentrated, and the other two becoming more male-dominated). Of the five occupations in which the female labour force increased relative to men, both clerical and sales were already strongly female-dominated. The occupations—administration, executive, managerial; and farmers, fishermen etc.—were very strongly male-dominated, and any relative increases of female numbers were small and had very little effect on the male concentrations. Thus, it appears that increases in women's employment have been mostly in those occupations already displaying a concentration of female workers, especially the clerical and sales occupations. This implies that the effect of women displacing men has only been slight. It is interesting to note that those occupations with high male concentrations had a decline in total employment. Hence, the three categories—farmers and fishermen etc.; transport and communication; and tradesmen, production process workers, miners and labourers etc.—all registered an absolute decrease in total labour force throughout the decade. This suggests that the decline in relative male employment may be due to declining demand for traditionally male occupations whereas increases in female employment may be due to increased demand for traditionally female occupations.[18]

Table 2.3 considers the relative growth rates of male and female employment for industries in aggregate. Of the twelve industries considered, women have increased their relative employment rates in six. Only two industries have female-concentrated work forces: community services; and recreation, personal, other services (women increased their numbers in the former and decreased in the latter). Of the remaining ten industries, all male-concentrated, women increased their relative position in eight. The industries that displayed increases in the employment rates of women were also those industries with the highest overall growth rates. Despite these increases in women's employment there was not a spectacular change in the gender mix of any particular industry with each industry showing only minor variation.

Summary

To reiterate, since the Second World War there has been a large relative increase in the labour force participation of women.[19] This growth was particularly strong during the 1960s. With the exception of 15–19 year olds all age groups of women have increased their participation rates since the 1960s, although this growth was especially noticeable in the 30–45 year age group. Women also showed a decreasing tendency to leave the labour market in the childbearing years of 25–35. Women increased both their full-time and part-time participation rates relative to men. Furthermore, women increased their share of total employment, as reflected by women increasing their aggregate hours of employment relative to men.

3

Segregation

Very few workplaces have the same proportion of men and women as that found in the total economy's labour force. We use the term *segregation* to refer to this disproportionate concentration of either men or women. According to the Macquarie dictionary,[1] *to segregate* is 'to separate or set apart from the others or from the main body; isolate'. This chapter studies the proportions of men and women working in the major occupations and industries. It will become apparent that most of these occupations and industries have either strongly concentrated male, or strongly concentrated female, work forces.

Five major aspects of male-female segregation are discussed: occupational segregation over the last 70 years, education and occupational segregation, segregation and female earnings relative to male earnings, industrial segregation and finally, Lewis's index of combined occupational and industrial segregation.[2]

Occupational segregation

According to Oppenheimer,[3] a disproportionately female (male) occupation occurs if women (men) form a higher proportion of workers in that occupation than they do in the total labour force. The explicit assumption is that women should be represented throughout all occupations in equal proportions to the female share of the total labour force. If it is found that women have a participation rate in an occupation that exceeds their share of the total labour force, it will

18

Table 3.1 Women in disproportionately female occupations, 1911–85

	Disproportionately female occupations		
Year	Females as a percentage of total labour force	Percentage of female labour force in these occupations	
		Expected	Observed
1911	20	23	84
1921	20	26	83
1933	23	22	74
1947	22	33	78
1961	25	32	80
1966	30	34	80
1971	32	39	82
1975	35	28	80
1980	37	30	81
1985	38	31	82

Source: Power (1975b), ABS (6101, 1986; 45)

be claimed that this reflects segregation of women into the occupation. For instance, *if* women make up 30 per cent of the total economy's labour force then according to this definition each occupation's workforce should be 30 per cent female and 70 per cent male. If the employment rate for women is found to be greater than 30 per cent, then women are being segregated into this occupation. Table 3.1[4] considers the extent of segregation within occupations, in terms of male and female ratios.

The first column of Table 3.1 presents the straightforward measure of women as a percentage of the total labour force for the economy. (It should be remembered that the labour force includes not only those people actually employed but also those seeking work.)[5] The proportion of the labour force that is female has increased significantly from 20 per cent in 1911 to become 38 per cent in 1985. This rapid increase in the participation rate for women is as would be expected from the conclusions of Chapter 2.[6]

Column two lists the percentage of women *expected* in the respective occupations, that is, the percentage of female labour *expected* in these occupations if the sex classification for occupations had been the *same* as the sexual composition of the total labour force.

Column three considers the percentage of the female labour force actually observed in those occupations that have been found to be disproportionately female. Thus, after ascertaining which occupations have a higher proportion of women than the proportion in the total economy's workforce, the actual number of women working in these occupations was estimated and found to be some 80 per cent of the female work force. This suggests that the great majority of women are concentrated into very few occupations and that, conversely, very few men occur in these occupations.

Table 3.1 reveals that female participation in the total labour force has increased greatly over the last 74 years. It can also be seen that close to 80 per cent of women work in occupations that are disproportionately female and that the extent of this segregation has remained remarkably stable over the 74-year span. Thus, despite large relative increases in female participation rates and employment rates,[7] there has been very little change in the occupations employing women between 1911 and 1985, or in the proportion of women that these occupations employ. This conclusion is supported by recent work[8] which found that, between 1966 and 1984, the occupational (and industrial) segregation of women actually increased.[9]

Considering the occupations in greater detail,[10] in 1975 and 1982 the occupations with disproportionately large numbers of female employees were; clerical with 68.3 per cent of its labour force female in 1975 and 70.6 per cent in 1982, service sport and recreation with 64.9 per cent and 63.0 per cent respectively, sales with 52.2 per cent and 59.8 per cent and professional technical with 42.5 per cent and 45.0 per cent. The corresponding female share in the total labour force was 34.6 per cent in 1975 and 36.7 per cent in 1982.

If the occupational groupings are broken up into smaller components it can be found that the segregation effect is even stronger. For example, 68.5 per cent of female professionals are either employed as nurses or teachers. There are no sub-divisions within the professional occupation that have a negligible number of male employees. Yet, there are negligible numbers[11] of female architects, engineers, surveyors, clergy, biologists, chemists, physicists, geologists, veterinarians and law professionals. In the service, sport and recreation occupation 59.7 per cent of women[12] are employed in the housekeeper, cook, maid and related worker group or they are employed as caretakers. If barmaids and waitresses are included this figure increases to 72.7 per cent of women.[13] Therefore, it would seem that the estimates of segregation in column 3 of Table 3.1 may actually underestimate the extent of occupational segregation facing women. Women appear in a minority of occupations and these female-dominated occupations tend to have a domestic role.

Segregation and earnings

To test the effect of occupational segregation on the female share of the total wage bill (the share of the economy's total wages that are going to women) a simple index, Rf, was devised. An *index* (or index number) is a ratio that is used to highlight a difference between groups. This index compares the difference in the wages that men and women earn due to their being located in different occupations.[14] The index is discussed in detail in the endnotes.[15]

When coarse occupational blockings for ten occupations were used[16] in calculating the index, it was found that the earnings received by women (if they are paid according to the male earning rate in each occupation) were 96.7 per cent of the total earnings received by men but, when the same index was calculated for a more detailed occupational listing of 45 occupations[17] it was found that total female earnings (that would be received if female earnings were equal to male earnings in each occupation) were only 62.6 per cent of male earnings. Thus, it was found that the total earnings of women were substantially lower than the total earnings of men due to the fact that women were concentrated in occupations that pay relatively lower wages than those occupations in which men are concentrated. If women's earnings are lower than men's earnings within each specific occupation, this effect will be even stronger.[18] It should be noted that finding this difference between male and female wages does not itself prove discrimination: for instance, it may be that women lack the required levels of education to be employed in the higher paid occupations.

Table 3.2   Occupation segregation by education/training attainment

| | Percentage of males/females in an occupation | | | | | |
| | Predicted | | Actual | | Ratio (%) | |
Occupation	M	F	M	F	M	F
Professional, technical						
etc.	64.6	35.4	54.5	45.5	84.4	128.5
Admin., exec., managerial	61.9	38.1	82.8	17.2	133.8	45.1
Clerical	60.8	39.2	26.9	73.1	44.2	186.5
Sales	60.5	39.5	45.8	54.2	75.7	137.2
Farmers, fishermen, timber						
getters etc.	60.7	39.3	74.8	25.3	123.2	64.4
Miners, quarrymen etc.	61.1	38.9	99.5	*	162.8	*
Transport, & communication	60.7	39.3	87.6	12.2	144.3	31.0
Tradesmen, prod. process,						
labourers, miners	61.7	38.3	87.8	12.0	62.1	31.3
Service, Sport, & Recreation	61.0	39.0	36.8	62.2	60.0	162.1

Source: ABS (6235, February 1986; 13)

Education and segregation

Does the occupational grouping of women merely reflect the educational levels of women? To consider this issue more fully Addison and Siebert's simple index has been adopted.[19] The aim here is to standardise for levels of general education. Thus, the index establishes the hypothetical occupational distribution that would occur if women of a given education level are located throughout occupations as are men with the same level of education. This hypothetical distribution is then compared with the distribution actually occurring. For a detailed description of the index being used see the endnotes.[20]

The first two columns of Table 3.2[21] present the percentage of men and women that should appear in an occupation, if general education is the only prerequisite to entry, given the present educational requirements of that occupation and the dispersion of this education level between men and women. The third and fourth columns list the percentage of men and women that actually do occur in that occupation and columns five and six give the ratio of the actual numbers to those predicted in percentage form. Thus, in the administrative, executive and managerial occupation there are a sufficient number of suitably educated women to fill 38.1 per cent of this workforce. Yet only 17.2 per cent of the occupation's workforce is female. The difference between these two figures cannot be explained in terms of sexual differences in levels of general education. Considering Table 3.2 in aggregate, it can be seen that the occupational distribution of both genders has little relevance to their level of general education.[22] Many highly-educated women appear in those occupations which do not require their education and many men, with relatively less education, fill those occupations that require, on average, higher education levels.[23] This pattern is also apparent in reverse. For instance, in the Sales occupation the average education level of the male employees is higher than the expected work force level. This suggests that females are occupying jobs within the sales occupation that require, on average, higher education levels than the women have. It can be concluded that differences in general education levels between the sexes do not explain the distribution of the gender groups between occupations. It can also be similarly argued, therefore, that the difference between the male and female wage bill is also far from fully explained by gender differences in general education levels.

Segregation by industry

Table 3.3[24] considers segregation by industry. This table is based on work previously carried out by Moir and Selby-Smith.[25] According to these authors the term *disproportionately female* refers to an industry where more than *50 per cent* of the work force is female. Obviously this differs from the Oppenheimer measure that was used for occupational segregation. In fact, the Moir and Selby-Smith measure is harder to satisfy than the Oppenheimer measure. Using the latter measure an industry would have been considered to be disproportionately female if it contained a greater proportion of women than occurred in the total labour force (some *40 per cent* in 1987).

Moir and Selby-Smith calculated which industries had disproportionately male, well represented, or disproportionately female work forces in 1977–78. They did not recalculate these figures for 1971–72; they assumed that the relative proportions of males and females in the industries' workforces had not changed over time. The figures pre-

Table 3.3 Industrial segregation of the labour force 1971–87

Industry status	Percentage of female labour force				Percentage of male labour force			
	1971–2	1977–8	1984	1987	1971–2	1977–8	1984	1987
Disproportionately female (>50% female)	56.1	60.7	60.4 (62.2)	60.2	15.4	19.0	25.1 (27.3)	26.2
Well-represented (20–50% female)	34.9	31.2	32.6 (30.8)	33.1	40.6	39.9	43.1 (40.9)	42.6
Disproportionately male (<20% female)	9.0	8.1	7.0 (7.0)	6.8	44.0	41.1	31.7 (31.7)	31.1

Source: Moir and Smith (1979), ABS (6203, 1984 and 1987)

sented in Table 3.3 (for 1971–72 and 1977–78) were estimated by summing the number of employees for each of these three different types of industries.

The bracketed values for 1984 were estimated by assuming that the disproportionately male, well represented, or disproportionately female industries had not changed since 1977–78. However, investigation found that the gender mix of the industries had changed over time: the property and business services industry changed from being disproportionately female to become well represented and the finance and investment industry moved from the well represented category to become disproportionately female. These were the only industries to change during the 1978–84 time period. The employment rates with the updated proportions of male and female workers are presented above the bracketed values in the column for 1984 of Table 3.3. There is very little difference between these values (bracketed and not bracketed) as would be expected given the minor movement in industries between the categories. The following list shows all industries according to the group or category they were estimated to be in during 1984.

Group one: disproportionately female work forces. These 10 industries are: knitting mills and clothing; footwear; retail trade; health; education, museums and libraries; welfare and religion; restaurants, hotels and clubs; private households employing staff; and finance and investment (which was in group two in 1977–78).

Group two: the well represented category. These thirteen industries are: food, beverage and tobacco; textiles; paper, printing and publishing; chemical, petroleum and coal products; other machinery and equipment; miscellaneous manufacturing; wholesale trade; air transport; other transport and storage; communication; insurance and services; entertainment and recreational services; and property and business services (which was in Group one in 1977–78).

Group three: the disproportionately male category. Industries consisted of: forestry and logging; fishing and hunting; road transport; railway transport; water transport; metallic minerals; oil and gas; other mining; non metallic mineral services; wood, wood products and furniture; base metal products; fabricated metal products; and transport equipment.

Table 3.3 is updated to include 1987. The values for 1987 were calculated using the industries that corresponded with the categories in 1987, rather than using the 1977–78 groupings of Moir and Selby-Smith. Between 1984 and 1987, the ABS substantially changed the industrial categories so these figures had to be recalculated.

Table 3.3 shows that women are more highly concentrated in the disproportionately female industries than men are concentrated in the disproportionately male industries. Thus, it can be found that in 1987, 26.2 per cent of the male labour force worked in industries which were disproportionately female and only 6.8 per cent of the female work force worked in industries that were disproportionately male. This means that men have a greater variety of industrial employment than do women. Furthermore, this trend can be seen to be increasing as the number of women being employed in male-dominated occupations has fallen from 9 per cent in 1971–72 to 6.8 per cent in 1987, while more men are finding work in the female-dominated occupations (15.4 per cent in 1971–72 to 26.2 per cent in 1987).

The proportion of the female work force in the disproportionately female industries is virtually twice as large as the proportion of the male work force in disproportionately male industries.[26] This means that the range of employment for women is relatively more limited than for men. The female-dominated industries employ a disproportionately large section of the economy's work force and appear to be increasing in their relative size as employers.[27]

Combined industrial and occupational segregation

So far it has been found that women are segregated in both occupation and industry categories. The extent of occupational and industrial segregation, however, has been considered separately. Occupational and industrial segregation are not discrete in the actual market place. Instead, workers carry out an occupation within a specific industry: for instance, a clerk in the agricultural industry or a tradesman in the manufacturing industry. To fully consider the extent of segregation we need to consider both industrial and occupational segregation simultaneously. Lewis[28] provides an index that can detect both of these kinds of segregation.

This index measures the percentages of men (or women) who would have to change occupations (or industries) so that the distribution of men (women) within the occupation (or industry) matches the gender mix in the total economy's work force. The index limits the difficulties encountered by crudely defined occupational classifications which can merge what are, in effect, different occupations, for instance, school teachers and doctors will both be considered as professionals. This combined index also enables consideration of the different rates of pay for the same occupation in different industries.

Table 3.4[29] lists Lewis's estimated indices for industrial, occupational and combined industrial and occupational segregation for 1891–1981. These indices are calculated using the Duncan-Duncan index[30] for industrial and occupational segregation. The column considering occupational segregation (S_i) shows that Lewis's measures can vary greatly according to the disaggregation of the occupational groupings. In other words, the larger the categories of occupations considered, the larger the occupational segregation found by the index.[31] This conclusion corresponds to our own findings discussed in occupational segregation. Changes in the indexes throughout time can be accredited to either composition or mix effects. The *composition effect* refers to a change in the proportions of men and women working in an occupation or industry over time. Thus, if the proportion of women in a workplace rises from 20 to 25 per cent then the composition of that workplace has changed. *Mix effects* occur when the proportion of men and women in a workplace changes because the structure of the actual workplace has changed. If more women are employed in banking it may not be that they are being employed as managers, accountants or even tellers. Rather, with the advent of computers, the actual structure of tasks in banking has changed over time and many of these women may be being employed as key punch operators. The analyst therefore needs to carefully distinguish between composition and mix effects.

Table 3.5 shows estimates of segregation (in percentages) using Lewis's equations. It reveals that segregation is falling, but only at a very slow rate. This rate is especially slow for occupational segregation. Lewis provides predictions of

28 Women working

Table 3.4 Segregation indices, 1891–1981 (in percentages)

Year	Female proportion of breadwinners Fp	Occupations n	Industries m	Occupational Si	Industrial Sj	Combined Sij
1891	0.20	7		47.5		
		36		67.8		
1901	0.22	7		46.7		
		36		66.5		
1911	0.20	7		44.7		
		36		69.6		
		102		71.4		
1921	0.20	7		45.8		
		37		65.8		
1933	0.26	10		46.8		
		39		62.5		
			10		45.8	
			40		62.1	
1945	0.28	9		46.2		
		63		62.0		
			9		35.6	
			50		50.5	
1947	0.22	8		40.7		
		207		64.3		
			10		40.7	
			53		53.2	
		8	10			55.5
1954	0.23		12		35.5	
			61		38.6	
1961	0.25	10		48.2		
		71		72.6		
			12		39.8	
			68		46.1	
1966	0.29	11		47.3		
		71		59.8		
			14		35.0	
1971	0.32	9		44.1		
		71		63.2		
			12		32.1	
			47		39.2	
1976	0.35	10		46.3		
		71		57.9		
			12		30.5	
		10	12			51.6
		71	12			59.6
1981		10		47.5		
		71		58.9		
		296		64.1		
			12		31.6	
			39		36.6	
			47		36.9	
			157		40.7	

Source: Lewis (1982), Lewis (1983)

Table 3.5   Predictions of segregation (in percentages)

Year	Estimated occupational segregation (n = 50) Si	Estimated industrial segregation (n = 50) Sj
1891	71.3	a
1901	65.0	a
1911	63.2	94.4
1921	62.2	76.8
1931	61.5	64.0
1941	60.9	55.5
1951	60.5	49.5
1961	60.1	44.9
1971	59.8	41.2
1981	59.5	38.2
1991	59.3	35.8
2001	59.0	33.7

Note: a Greater than 100
Source: Lewis (1982)

segregation levels up to the year 2001. He expects occupational segregation to fall by only 0.5 per cent in the twenty years between 1981 and 2001, with industrial segregation falling by a larger 4.5 per cent. There is some contention as to the legitimacy of Lewis's findings. Some authors[32] claim that Lewis's results do not predict future movements in the labour market because Lewis does not allow the market to adapt to changes in circumstances. If Lewis's estimates are correct, normal market forces could be expected to have very little effect on occupational segregation within the next twenty years. The implication being that if the society wants to lower occupational segregation then it cannot rely on market forces. Implementation of change may involve direct action either in the form of anti-discrimination legislation and/or affirmative action policies.

Summary

Women were found to be highly concentrated within occupations that are disproportionately female. This occupational segregation appears to have remained remarkably stable between 1911 and 1985. Furthermore, this segregation was linked to women receiving lower average earnings than men, and the segregation did not appear to be related to sexual differences in general education.

Segregation by industry was less obvious than segregation by occupation. However, industries were significantly segregated with women being concentrated in female-dominated industries and very few women appearing in the male-dominated industries. The industrial segregation of women had the effect of severely limiting the employment range of women relative to men. Female dominated industries were found to employ a disproportionately large sector of the total labour force and to be increasing their employment relative to the disproportionately male industries with their small, almost totally male, labour forces.

Finally, Lewis's study revealed that segregation by both occupation and by industry are decreasing over time, though at a very slow pace (especially for occupational segregation). In effect, market mechanisms cannot be relied upon to remove segregation except in the very long run. The implication being that more direct action may be necessary to implement the removal of segregation.

4

Wages and earnings

Wages and earnings are important for any member of our society, we all want to be paid well for the work that we do. This chapter concentrates on differences in wages and earnings between men and women. It should be noted that 'award wages' and 'earnings' are not necessarily the same for a worker. In simple terms, an *award* wage is an amount specified by one of the government operated statutory authorities (such as the Federal Arbitration Commission) as the *minimum* wage that should be paid to an employee carrying out a certain task. Many employees will be paid *above* the required minimum wage. The amount they actually receive is referred to as their *earnings*. As we shall find, there is often a very substantial difference between the award wage and the employee's earnings.

Another point worth considering at this stage is what the wage should be set equal to; should it equal the worker's productivity, the worker's needs, some socially set level (consistent with relative wage levels in the community), some proportion of the firm's profits? Orthodox economic theory (in Australia) typically claims that the wage rate should be set to reflect the value of the worker's productivity for the employer. Thus, if the worker produces more units (for instance the carpenter makes more chairs or the storeman packs more shelves) or if the price (the value) of the final units (the chairs or shelved stock) rises then the worker could expect a wage rise. If, on the other hand, some outside factor (such as trade union pressure or government legislation) forces the wage rate up without the value of the worker's productivity rising then orthodox economic theory predicts that the employer will respond by laying off work-

31

ers. In other words, increasing the wage rate without simultaneously increasing the value of the worker's productivity will lead to an increase in unemployment.

This chapter begins by examining the differences for men and women in earnings and award wages since 1914, concentrating on wage and employment changes for women relative to men within three industries since 1966. Secondly, it discusses sexual differences in wages in the Australian public service throughout the 1970s and the difficulties in testing models[1] with Australian data. Thirdly, it considers gender based differences in promotion in the private and public work force and its implications for relative earnings. And, finally, it takes an overall approach to many of the factors that influence relative wages.

Relative earnings, wages and employment

Table 4.1 is an updated version of a table by Gregory and Duncan.[2] Column two presents an index of relative female to male minimum awards across the aggregated economy from 1914 to 1987. It can be seen that in 1914 the average award wage for women was only half (49.3 per cent) of the average award wage for men. By 1987 this ratio had risen so that the average award wage for women was 92.7 per cent of that for men.

The award wage of women relative to men was comparatively stable throughout the 73-year period (1914–87) with the exception of two phases; 1939–50 and 1969–77.[3] The increase in relative female awards in these phases can be linked to changes in the attitudes of the state and federal wage tribunals, which determine award wages in Australia. Before the Second World War, occupations were determined to be either 'male' or 'female' according to which gender dominated in that occupation's work place. Male occupations were then paid a 'male minimum wage' which was set at a level believed, by the Tribunal, to be required to support a man, his wife and children in a civilised community. Female occupations were paid the 'female minimum wage' which was the amount believed to be required to support a single woman, and was set at 54 per cent of the minimum male wage (the implication was that only men were re-

Table 4.1 Ratio of female to male earnings (in percentages)

Year	Award rates Females/males	Earnings Females/males	Earning ratio /Award ratio
1914	49.3	n.a.	n.a
1939	53.6	n.a.	n.a
1950	69.5	n.a.	n.a
1954	70.1	n.a.	n.a
1964	72.0	59.2	82.2
1966	71.0	57.8	81.4
1967	72.4	58.2	80.4
1968	71.0	57.0	80.3
1969	72.0	58.4	81.1
1970	73.2	59.1	80.7
1971	74.6	60.7	81.4
1972	77.4	64.3	83.1
1973	79.4	65.9	83.0
1974	85.2	70.9	83.2
1975	90.8	75.7	83.4
1976	92.4	77.1 (79.6)	83.4 (86.1)
1977	93.3	76.6 (81.0)	82.1 (86.8)
1978	92.4	(81.8)	(88.5)
1979	91.8	(80.3)	(87.5)
1980	91.6	(79.6)	(86.9)
1981	92.0	(80.1)	(87.1)
1982	91.6	(81.9)	(89.4)
1983	91.6	(82.3)	(89.8)
1984	91.8	n.a	n.a
1985	91.9	(82.4)	(89.7)
1986	92.3	(82.6)	(89.5)
1987	92.7	n.a	n.a

Note: Award wage indices base averaged quarterly wage, 1976.
Sources: 1914–77 Gregory and Duncan (1981), ABS (6101, 1983, 1985), ABS (6306, May 1986; 22), ABS (6312, May 1987; 5)

quired to support a family). The criteria the tribunals used when setting these early basic wages was a suitable standard of living for the working classes rather than a measure of workers' respective productivities.

During the Second World War the Women's Employment Board was devised and eventually established in 1942. The Board aimed at encouraging women into the labour force and lessening the discrepancy between male and female wages. The Board claimed that female workers were some 60–100 per cent as productive as male workers (depending on the occupation) and should be paid this higher wage. The differential was claimed to be due to women having higher levels of turnover and absenteeism as well as a comparative

lack of physical strength. While the suggestions of the
Women's Employment Board were not fully implemented,
their suggestions corresponded, in time, to the relative increase in the female minimum award wage between 1939
and 1950. The Women's Board based its argument on productivity unlike the tribunals which based their findings on
the argument that the working classes should enjoy a decent
standard of living (the 'need' criteria).

In 1950 the federal tribunal set wages in female occupations at 75 per cent of the male minimum wage. Wage
relativities between men and women then remained very
stable until 1969.[4] On 19 June 1969, the federal tribunal
introduced 'equal pay for equal work' to be fully implemented by 1 January 1971. The inherent justification for
this legislation was that employees of equal productivity
should be paid an equal wage. However, difficulties arose
with the interpretation of this legislation. Since women
tend to work in segregated occupations and industries, it
was difficult to argue that women were actually performing
the *equal work* of men. The legislation was strengthened[5] in
1972 when the tribunal introduced 'equal pay for work of
equal value', enabling women in highly concentrated female
occupations to also seek wage comparity. The equal pay
initiative was to be implemented in three equal stages up
until 1975 when (it was hoped) gender based wage dispari-
ties would have become negligible. Table 4.1 suggests that
the legislation appears to have had considerable influence
during the period 1969–77. During this time the female
minimum award wage rose from being some 72 per cent of
the male minimum award wage in 1969 to almost 92 per
cent by 1976. There has been little gain in the relative
female award wage since 1976, rather, the ratio of the
female to male award wage has fluctuated around the 92
per cent level for the past eleven years.

In 1985, the Australian Council of Trade Unions (ACTU)
lodged a test case in which it argued that the concept of
'equal pay for equal work' should be equated with that of
'comparable worth'. Men and women are typically employed in different occupations, many of which will require
similar skill levels and responsibilities (and are therefore
comparable) although strictly speaking the occupations are
not identical (or equal). If the federal tribunal was to adopt

(margin notes) EP 1971   EP 1972

the ACTU's case, then it would be possible for workers in female-dominated occupations to have their work valued against workers in male-dominated (or in well represented) occupations. American studies[6] suggest that the adoption of comparative worth legislation should lead to a significant increase in the earnings of women relative to men. The case was rejected by the federal tribunal, which argued that using 'comparable worth' as a criterion for wage comparisons would be 'inappropriate and confusing'.[7] Furthermore the adoption of the comparative worth criteria would 'strike at the heart of accepted methods of wage fixation in this country and would be particularly destructive of the present Wage Fixing Principles'.[8] The federal tribunal's rejection of the comparable worth claim may[9] represent a major drawback for the Women's Movement.

The likely result of the rejection of 'comparable worth' is that the path towards a situation of equal economic status between male and female workers will be slower. Moreover, by not providing a relatively easy means whereby pay and conditions can be improved in female-dominated occupations, incentives do not exist for men to enter 'female' occupations and thereby break them down.[10]

Column three of Table 4.1 lists the ratio of average, full-time, non-managerial female earnings to average full-time non-managerial male earnings, between 1964 and 1976. These earnings refer to private sector employees only. From 1976 the earnings are for combined private and public sector employees.[11] These values are placed in brackets to signify the discrepancy and a two-year overlap is provided. Given this discrepancy in the data, a similar trend appears to be occurring in the earnings ratio as was found for the ratio of minimum award wages. Hence there was a comparatively stable period during 1964 to 1969 and then a rapid increase until 1976 when the ratio virtually stabilised again at the new, substantially higher rate. The overall earnings of women has shown significant gain between the mid-sixties and mid-eighties: in 1966 women received on average 57.8 per cent of the average male earnings, by 1986 this had increased to become 82.6 per cent of male earnings.

The earnings ratio reflects the ratio of the actual wages received by men and women. Award wages are the *legal* minimum wage for a task, and earnings are the wages *actually* paid for that task. As can be seen, in column three of Table 4.1, the earnings ratio for women is substantially lower than the award ratio. In 1964 the earnings ratio was some 12.8 percentage points lower than the award ratio; by 1986 the difference between the ratios had decreased but the earnings ratio for women was still 9.7 percentage points below the award ratio. This shows that women are in reality receiving much less in wages than the ratio of legal minimum wages would suggest, implying that men are reaping more in 'over-award' payments than are women.[12] These extra payments may not necessarily be due to employers paying men more but may also be linked to the types of occupations and industries that men work in.[13] It is also interesting to note that the increase in the ratio of earnings between 1969 and 1976 was very similar to the increase in the ratio of award wages in the same period; the ratio of award wages increasing by 22.3 per cent while the ratio of earnings increased by 22 per cent. This finding would seem to deny the simplistic argument that extra payments occur in certain occupations or industries due to productivity levels. Instead, it would appear there is a strong force in the labour market to perpetuate the gap between the award wage and the actual amount earned.

Turning to column four of Table 4.1, the ratio of earnings to award wages from 1964 to 1987 shows very little fluctuation, even when award wages rose so significantly in the early seventies. This supports our finding that earnings adjust to increases in the award wage so as to maintain the level of above award payments.

Table 4.2[14] presents similar information to Table 4.1, but here the analysis is limited to a study of three industries from 1966 to 1987. Consideration of changes in male and female employment within these industries is included. Thus in the food, beverage and tobacco industry, female award rates increased greatly, relative to male award rates between 1969 and 1976, balancing thereafter. Female earnings relative to male earnings rose by a similar proportion in the same period, and the ratio of earnings to wages remained around 82 per cent throughout. These are the same results found in Table 4.1 but it is very interesting to note that the ratio of female employment to

Table 4.2 Ratio of female/male award wages and earnings for selected industry groups

Year	Food, Beverages, Tobacco					Textiles, Clothing, Footwear					Engineering, Metals, Vehicles				
	Aw. f/m Ar %	Earn. f/m Er %	Er/Ar %	females/all	Employment ratio index	Aw. f/m Ar %	Earn. f/m Er %	Er/Ar %	females/all	Employment ratio index	Aw. f/m Ar %	Earn. f/m Er %	Er/Ar %	females/all	Employment ratio index
1966	70.2	58.5	83.3	0.25	100.0	70.7	58.6	82.9	0.66	100.0	71.8	55.9	77.9	0.14	100.0
1967	70.9	58.9	83.1	0.25	100.5	72.2	59.5	82.4	0.66	101.8	72.8	55.3	76.0	0.15	104.0
1968	71.3	58.9	82.6	0.26	104.6	71.7	58.3	81.3	0.66	101.4	70.1	53.9	76.9	0.15	108.6
1969	71.7	59.0	82.3	0.26	110.7	72.2	59.3	82.1	0.66	101.6	72.9	56.5	77.5	0.15	114.9
1970	72.1	59.5	82.5	0.27	116.9	71.9	58.0	80.7	0.66	102.9	77.6	60.4	77.8	0.16	122.8
1971	73.9	61.2	82.8	0.27	121.8	75.4	60.2	79.8	0.66	98.0	81.9	63.3	77.3	0.16	126.3
1972	74.9	63.6	84.9	0.26	123.2	74.1	60.6	81.8	0.67	95.1	85.3	66.5	78.0	0.18	120.4
1973	81.3	66.4	81.7	0.26	122.0	81.0	61.4	75.8	0.67	92.9	89.5	66.4	74.2	0.19	134.4
1974	90.1	70.2	78.7	0.28	129.0	87.9	71.0	80.8	0.67	91.4	92.1	71.7	77.9	0.21	152.2
1975	92.7	74.8	80.7	0.28	123.6	93.1	74.8	90.3	0.66	73.5	96.8	75.8	78.3	0.20	120.5
1976	93.7	76.3	81.4	0.27	119.1	93.8	76.1	81.1	0.66	75.5	97.3	74.5	76.6	0.20	118.9
1977	94.2	76.7	81.4	0.26	117.4	95.6	75.8	79.3	0.66	70.1	97.3	75.0	77.1	0.19	118.0
1978	94.1	77.2	82.0	n.a	n.a	94.0	76.9	81.8	n.a	n.a	98.2	77.0	78.4	n.a	n.a
1979	93.1	81.8	87.9	n.a	n.a	93.4	76.1	81.5	n.a	n.a	96.3	74.6	77.5	n.a	n.a
1980	93.7	77.5	82.7	n.a	n.a	94.3	71.5	75.8	n.a	n.a	97.1	75.1	77.3	n.a	n.a
1981	93.3	80.4	86.2	n.a	n.a	92.0	71.3	77.5	n.a	n.a	96.9	76.4	78.8	n.a	n.a
1982	94.0	n.a	n.a	n.a	n.a	93.8	n.a	n.a	n.a	n.a	97.1	n.a	n.a	n.a	n.a
1983	93.9	77.7	82.7	n.a	n.a	93.7	76.8	82.0	n.a	n.a	97.1	77.8	80.1	n.a	n.a
1984	93.8	n.a	n.a	n.a	n.a	93.5	n.a	n.a	n.a	n.a	97.0	n.a	n.a	n.a	n.a
1985	94.0	81.6	86.8	n.a	n.a	93.5	79.6	85.1	n.a	n.a	97.2	78.0	80.2	n.a	n.a
1986	94.0	80.9	86.1	n.a	n.a	n.a	74.5	n.a	n.a	n.a	97.1	77.2	79.5	n.a	n.a
1987	93.9	n.a	n.a	n.a	n.a	n.a	n.a	n.a	n.a	n.a	98.2	n.a	n.a	n.a	n.a

Note: All data up to and including 1977 from Gregory and Duncan (1981). Award wages 1978–86 taken from December of the year, 1987 taken from May data. All data uses the 1976 base index used by Gregory and Duncan (1981). Earnings 1978–87 taken from May of the year. Award wages for 1986–87 for Textiles, Clothing & Footwear industry n.a due to change in ABS categories. From 1977 the Engineering, Metals, Vehicles group was reclassified as 'Total Metal Products'.

Sources: Gregory and Duncan, 1981, ABS (6101, 1982, 1984, 1985), ABS (6312 May 1987; 6). ABS (6306, May 1986; 22).

male employment was remarkably stable throughout the time period, never varying by more than two percentage points from 26 per cent (despite the very significant increase in female earnings relative to male earnings that occurred during this period). This appears to contradict the predictions of orthodox economic theory because the award wage for women was not increased due to an increase in the productivity of women but due to social pressure for equity. As discussed previously, if the wage rate rises without a productivity gain we could expect the employer to respond by laying off those employees. In each of the three industry groups studied the relative earnings of women to men rose almost 20 percentage points between 1966 and 1976 and yet the employment ratios for women in each industry showed very little change. This phenomenon raises some interesting questions as to what criteria employers use when setting wage levels.

Wage differentials and the public service

Turning now to consider gender based wage differentials in the Australian public service, Bruce Chapman[15] provides a rare study of sexual differences in wages within an occupation (the clerical administrative division). The great value of Chapman's study is that it follows the progression of a specific group of employees in 1969, 1973 and 1979. This is a vast improvement on the usual Australian studies which can only discuss worker characteristics in averaged terms. Chapman's estimates hold constant the influence of education, on-the-job experience and general labour market experience, thus allowing the analyst to focus more closely on the effects of sexual and regional differences on salaries.[16]

Human capital is a term used to discuss the level of skills (both general education skills and job specific education skills) that a worker has acquired. Chapman uses the conventional human capital function to measure the roles of general labour market experience, on-the-job experience and education as salary determinants.[17] Chapman's analysis attempts to find what differences there are between male and female wages once allowances are made for any differences in their skills. We have reproduced Chapman's equations in the endnotes[18] for those readers interested.

Table 4.3 Average annual salaries by year ($)

Year		1969	1974	1979
Males	Canberra	5547	12421	19260
	Non-Canberra	4254	9720	15417
Females	Canberra	3750	10310	16450
	Non-Canberra	2975	8522	13654

Source: Chapman (1984a, 1984b)

Table 4.4 Predicted average salaries if females had been rewarded as males

Year	1969		1974		1979	
	Canberra	Non-Canberra	Canberra	Non-Canberra	Canberra	Non-Canberra
Actual	3750	2975	10310	8522	16450	13654
Predicted	4381	3481	11186	8930	17813	14501
Percentage Difference	15.52	15.68	8.15	4.68	7.96	6.02

Source: Chapman (1984b)

Table 4.3[19] presents the initial salary differential between the public servants in the clerical administrative division who were tested. It can be seen that Canberra employees had higher salaries than employees based in State branches and men had higher salaries than women in both Canberra and State offices.

The final estimating equation predicts a wage rate that would be paid to a group if, given the group's actual level of measurable human capital, it had been paid the same returns to this human capital stock as the alternative group. These values are listed in row two of Table 4.4.[20] Row one presents the actual female salaries and row three shows the percentage difference in salaries of men and women that cannot be explained by differences in general or specific education levels. Between 1969 and 1974 this unexplained salary differential decreased significantly; by almost a half in Canberra and two-thirds in the States. But, in the 1974–79 period this trend reversed with the percentage difference increasing slightly. It can be concluded that Chapman's

Table 4.5   Experience adjusted predicted average salaries if females had been rewarded as males

Year	1969		1974		1979	
	Canberra	Non-Canberra	Canberra	Non-Canberra	Canberra	Non-Canberra
Actual	3750	2975	10310	8522	16450	13654
Predicted	4079	3286	10949	8822	17682	14308
Percentage Difference	8.40	9.93	6.01	3.46	7.22	4.68

Source: Chapman (1984)

study found a significant salary differential between male and female employees that was not explained by human capital.

Chapman then restricts his analysis by claiming that the general labour market experience variable may overstate the actual general labour market experience for women if women have less continuous labour force participation than men. In other words, if women have spent less time in their jobs than the men have, women may have acquired less job specific skills. Chapman replaces the general labour market experience variable with an estimate of female participation within the clerical administrative group studied. He estimates the ratio of women that left during the ten-year period of the study to all the women involved in the study and then compares this to a similar ratio for the men. With this new estimate of the female general labour market variable the previous calculations are made again.[21] These findings are reproduced in Table 4.5.[22] Interestingly, using the new estimate for female experience makes little difference to the results found: the results for 1974 and 1979 are very similar in Tables 4.4 and 4.5, although the unexplained differential for 1969 falls. Table 4.5 shows that men are still receiving a significant salary differential that cannot be explained in terms of educational differences (either general or job specific).

Although there may be difficulties with the use of regression testing such as that used by Chapman,[23] and others,[24] Chapman's conclusion is quite clear: within the clerical administrative division of the Australian public service, men's wages are significantly higher than women's wages; this differential cannot be fully explained by gender differences in education.

Promotion

We could expect that discriminatory practices concerning promotional opportunities will have significant effects on relative earnings. If women receive less promotion, they will appear in the lower paid jobs in occupations or industries. While many authors discuss the presence of 'short promotional ladders' for women and the effect of sexual discrimination on promotion,[25] there appears to be little available Australian data. Nevertheless, it is possible to consider some of the implications of discrimination in promotion.

First, many of the top level promotions reside within the administrative, executive and managerial occupation category. Yet, in Chapter 2 of this study, 'Participation' (see Table 2.2), it was found that this category was one of the most highly male-concentrated occupations in the 1975–80 time period with a male concentration of 86.4 per cent.

Within this five-year period (1975–80) the total labour force of this category increased by 11.9 per cent. Women took up 34 per cent of these new jobs, while men absorbed the remaining 65.8 per cent. This increase in female employment created a growth of 2.5 percentage points in the total female labour force within the category. In the 1980–85 period this category grew 13.9 per cent, 46.6 per cent of these new jobs went to women and 53.5 per cent were taken by men. This led to a large increase in the female labour force of 11.4 percentage points, but only a small decrease in the overall male concentration of 0.2 percentage points causing the overall male concentration to fall to 82.3 per cent. Thus, the administrative, executive and managerial occupation is very highly male concentrated and has shown little increase in relative female employment throughout the seventies and early eighties.

Data concerning public service promotion is more readily available. Table 4.6[26] shows that in June 1983 there were no female department heads out of 31 possible positions. By December 1985[27] a female secretary to department had been employed, the remaining 30 heads were male. There were

Table 4.6   Full-time staff employed under the Public Service Act by category and division, June 1983ᵃ

Category	Permanent officers		Temporary employees		Exempt employees	
Division	Total number	Women as %	Total number	Women as %	Total number	Women as %
First	31	0.0	–	–	–	–
Second	1310	2.3	21	4.7	22	4.5
Third	69564	26.8	1847	41.0	343	25.9
Fourth	59837	50.8	5241	67.2	20974	25.9
Sub-total	130742	37.5	7109	60.2	21339	24.9
Total	....		159190	36.8	....	

Note: ᵃ For updated values see discussion on pp. 41–42
Source: Affirmative action for women vol II. p. 16

only 30 female second division officers out of a possible 1300 positions in 1983, by 1985 this had increased to 88 out of 1551. Women make up the majority of the lowest division of the full-time workers and they represent the vast majority of part-time workers. Hence, it appears that while women made up some 36.8 per cent of the total public service work force in 1983 and 39.6 per cent in 1985, these women are disproportionately concentrated in the lowest divisions and part-time employment. Women show very little success in rising above the third division. Much of the dearth of high level female public servants may be explained by previous discriminatory practices such as placing men above women of similar qualifications on application lists and removing permanency from women when they married.[28] These practices have been banned since the early 1970s and yet there are still few women employed above the third division.

This analysis suggests that women are finding little promotion in either the public service or in the private sector. This is supported by the scant numbers of women in the administrative, executive or managerial occupation or in the first or second division of the public service.[29] However, there is not sufficient data to consider differences in actual job ladders facing men and women nor any of the characteristics (horizontal and vertical movements, average worker age by position, etc.) of these labour markets.

Table 4.7 **Part-time staff employed by government departments by division, June 1983ᵃ**

Division	Total no. employees	Women as % of part-time employees
Second	–	–
Third	426	73.9
Fourth	2584	89.7
Total	3010	87.5

Note: ᵃ For updated values see discussion on pp. 41–42
Source: Affirmative action for women vol II. p. 17

An overall approach

There are many possible explanations for wage differences between men and women. A recent study undertaken by Chapman and Mulvey[30] investigated the relationship between the wages received by men and women and some of the more obvious variables (union membership, education, experience, region, country of birth, industry or occupation and marital status) that would affect this wage. This study is particularly valuable because it considers the effects of these variables on the wage rate *simultaneously*.

Chapman and Mulvey[31] focused on full-time employees who had only one job. This restriction left them with quite a large sample of 8946 men and 4330 women. They found that: 'If women had been rewarded for their measured human capital levels and other variables in the same way as men...then, other things being equal, they would have earned...13.07 per cent more than they did earn'.[32] Thus, some 13 per cent of the difference between male and female wages cannot be explained by the commonly accepted justifications for wage differences. '*The results imply that it is the differential employer treatment of women and men that explains sex differences in wages—measured variable differences between the sexes are seemingly unimportant.*'[33] Once the differences between men and women in education, job experience, nationality, trade union membership, occupation and industry, marital status and even the residential location of workers, have been taken into consideration there is still a significant unexplained wage differential between the sexes. This suggests that the resultant wage differential can be attributed to discrimination by employers against female employees. To reiterate, 'it is the differential employer treatment of women and men that explains sex differences in wages'.[34]

Summary

Female wages increased dramatically during the 1940s and the early 1970s in response to direct actions by tribunals to increase the female wage relative to the male wage. Wage relativities between men and women stabilised again between these periods. From 1969 onwards the ratio of male earnings to female earnings remained remarkably stable as did the ratio of female employment to male employment.

From Chapman's study of the clerical administrative division of the Australian public service, the differential between male and female wages could not be explained by sexual differences in education. Public service employers appeared to practice discrimination in favour of male employees, although the effect of this discrimination lessens with the length of time women spend in the occupation. It appears that women were receiving little promotion in the public service or private sector, but we need more data to investigate the promotion paths of women more fully.

Finally, a valuable study undertaken by Chapman and Mulvey found that, even after allowing for the major explanations provided for women receiving less wages than men, the female wage was still some 13 per cent lower than the male wage. This difference in wages cannot be explained by economically valid differences between the sexes but was instead due to women being discriminated against.

5

Turnover and absenteeism

Turnover and absenteeism both directly affect the number of days a worker spends with an employer. The period of tenure (or length of time spent in a job) can have a substantial affect on the wage paid. One of the most obvious reasons for this relationship is that an employer will not want to spend money on training an employee who is expected to leave. Similarly, promotion opportunities will typically go to those workers who have spent time in a workplace accumulating experience and the trust of the employer. Do women have significantly shorter periods of tenure than men; and can this explain much of the wage difference between men and women?

Absenteeism will also affect the wage of the employee. An employer might understandably react to an employee with high rates of absenteeism by setting a lower wage. If women are found to have higher rates of absenteeism, this might provide an explanation for the relatively smaller earnings women receive. The reader should be aware at this point of a practice called *statistical discrimination*. Statistical discrimination occurs when *all* members of a group are considered to behave the way the group may behave on the whole. Thus, if it is found that women on the whole have shorter rates of tenure, this does not necessarily mean that a specific woman will not stay in her job.

Discussion within this chapter is split into two parts. The first part concentrates on three issues:

1   the average length of tenure within a job, in months, of men and women since 1972;
2   the effect of occupational segregation on turnover;

3 employers' inaccurate estimates of male and female tenure.

The second part focuses on: absenteeism, specifically differences between male and female absenteeism, and the relationship between absenteeism and occupation.

Turnover

Table 5.1[1] presents the average length of female tenure (in months) compared to the average length of male tenure. The final row of the table presents the ratio of average female tenure to average male tenure (in percentage). Thus it can be found from the table that average female tenure was shorter than average male tenure in all of the years between 1972 and 1986 but the average length of tenure for women shows a much larger growth rate than does the length of tenure for men over this period. This results in a situation where women have increased their relative length of tenure from being 76.8 per cent of the length of the average male tenure in 1972 to become 86.1 per cent in 1986. However, the strong growth of female tenure in the late seventies seems to have levelled out in the mid-eighties (it has actually fallen from 88.6 per cent in 1983 to 86.1 per cent in 1986). This suggests that the length of female tenure may not catch up to male tenure, or at least not in the short run. It should be noted that the data used for Table 5.1 contains little information: from it, it is not possible to consider the working lives of any individual or even a specific group of women. Studies[2] have found that with greater detail, the relative tenure rate of women increases significantly. 'To isolate a pure sex differential one needs, ideally, microdata which allow adjustment for all the personal and job characteristics influencing turnover'.[3]

Table 5.2 considers turnover by occupation. The data used to calculate Table 5.2 is noticeably different to that used to calculate Table 5.1[4], hence the different overall tenure rates for 1983. Of the data used for Table 5.1 the longest period of tenure considered was 5 years and over, which was set at 60 months for our measures. However, for Table 5.2 the longest period considered was 10 years and over, set at 120 months. The inclusion of this longer time period increased average

Table 5.1 Average job tenure for males and females, 1972–83

Average job tenure (months)	February											Change from 72–86
	1972	1975	1976	1979	1980	1981	1982	1983	1984	1985	1986	
Male	38.4	39.5	39.0	38.2	39.2	37.7	37.8	38.7	39.7	38.9	38.3	-0.1
Female	29.5	30.5	32.2	33.1	34.1	32.7	33.2	34.3	34.8	34.0	32.9	3.4
Ratio f/m %	76.8	77.2	82.6	86.7	87.0	86.7	87.8	88.6	87.7	87.5	86.1	9.3

Source: ABS (6101, 1983, 1986)

Table 5.2 Average job tenure by occupation for February 1983

Average job tenure (months)	Prof. & tech.	Admin. exec. & manag.	Clerical	Sales	Farm., fish etc.	Trans. & comm.	Trade prod. nec.	Serv. sport & rec.	Total
Male	57.0	59.5	53.7	41.9	72.9	61.0	57.0	48.2	57.2
Female	46.9	52.1	45.2	38.1	73.9	52.5	49.7	45.2	46.6
% of occup'n female	45.1	13.8	70.9	56.4	23.8	14.1	11.6	61.9	37.2

Source: ABS (6209, 1983)

male tenure relative to average female tenure, thereby leading to a fall in overall female tenure relative to male tenure from 88.6 per cent in Table 5.1 to 81.5 per cent in Table 5.2 for 1983. In other words, more men stay with the same employer for more than 10 years than do women. This result is reflected in the lower values of the relative length of tenure for women. This effect was excluded from the estimates in Table 5.1 because data from the longer period was not available for all years. The longer period was included in Table 5.2 so that available information would be maximised.

Table 5.2 illustrates that the occupations with the shortest tenure for *both men and women* are also the occupations that have the highest concentrations of female employees. In order to consider the effect of occupational segregation on relative length of tenure a simple index[5] was devised to measure relative tenure if men and women were represented in each occupation according to their proportions in the economy's total labour force. The hypothetical female (male) occupational labour force is then multiplied by the respective female (male) tenure for the occupation, summed across all occupations and measured relative to a similar total for men (women). The effect of a larger male labour force for the economy as a whole is then weighted out and the resultant index is found.

For 1983 the index was found to be 88.1 per cent. Including the effect of occupational segregation, women are on average found to have tenure that is 88.1 per cent the length of average male tenure. The equivalent value prior to considering the effect of occupational segregation was 81.5 per cent, thus 6.6 percentage points, of the different lengths of tenure between men and women may be explained by segregation by occupation. But the data set used only enabled consideration of the main occupational blockings. These blockings are very coarse and ignore much of the extent of occupational segregation.[6] The difference in tenure may become considerably smaller if more detailed occupational categories were available.[7]

Lewis[8] provides an interesting study of turnover in which he found, via a series of interviews with personnel directors, that employers consistenly *underestimate* the quit rates of their male employees while simultaneously overestimating

Table 5.3   **Persons working: average number of days lost from work per person concerned by age by sex, 1983**

No. of days lost in last two weeks	Age by years			
	15–24	25–44	45 or more	Total
Males	0.25	0.24	0.34	0.27
Females	0.31ᵃ	0.25	0.31	0.28

Note: ᵃ Data liable to large statistical error due to small sample group.
Source: ABS (4311, 1983; 40)

the quit rates of their female employees. These estimates by employers can become self-fulfilling prophecies if women are channelled into lower paying, less satisfying work tasks which are associated with higher turnover levels. 'An occasional retreat from a boring job into unpaid housework is undoubtedly refreshing for women who can afford such a luxury.'[9] Lewis's study is of special interest since, if employers are consistently forming biased estimates of relative tenure for men and women, this may be because employers are unable to form the economically rational estimates which are necessary to validate statistical discrimination and employment techniques. In other words, employers may not be able to accurately estimate the relative tenure rates for men and women. If this is the case, there is a need for government intervention to ensure that employers are provided with more accurate information.

Absenteeism

Turning to absenteeism, there has been a noticeable lack of both Australian studies[10] and Australian data[11] on this subject. There is, however, at least one ABS survey[12] which, while published for 1977–78 and partially updated for 1983, does provide some useful information. In Table 5.3,[13] the average man can be seen to have had less days absent from work in the two weeks prior to being interviewed than did the average woman (0.27 and 0.28 days respectively). However, the only age group where women had a substantially longer period of absenteeism than men was in the 15–24 year bracket, and these figures are liable to large statistical error due to the small number of respondents. In

Table 5.4   Persons aged 15 years or more who are working: days lost from work in the two weeks before interview by occupation

Occupation	Number of days lost				% who lost days
	None	One	2–3	4–14	
Prof., Tech. etc.	746.8	36.0	19.44	17.7	9.70
Admin., Exec. etc.	284.8	6.9	2.9	4.2	5.80
Clerical Workers	849.3	44.0	28.1	14.5	10.27
Sales Workers	504.7	18.2	11.4	8.9	8.62
Farmers, Fisher etc.	382.6	8.9	5.4	6.7	6.15
Miners, Quarry etc.	39.4	a	a	3.5	10.65
Trans. & Commun.	272.1	10.8	8.6	9.5	10.55
Trades, Prod. etc.	1569.6	70.4	48.6	56.1	11.19
Serv. Sports etc.	469.8	16.5	10.2	15.0	9.75
Armed Services	32.1	a	a	a	9.32
Total	5200.1	213.8	136.5	138.4	

Note: ª Data liable to large statistical error due to small sample group.
Source: ABS (4321 1981; 15)

the major childbearing years (of 25–44 years) women showed very little difference in absenteeism to men; 0.24 days lost in the fortnight for men and 0.25 days lost for women. This is a particularly interesting result since it is often argued that women need to take more days off work to care for sick children. For the 44 and over bracket, women were found to have less absenteeism (0.34 days for men and 0.31 days for women).

Absenteeism may be linked to many factors, such as the degree of physical difficulty associated with certain tasks or, job satisfaction.[14] Much of the explanation for the absenteeism may be due to segregation by occupation. In Table 5.4[15] it can be seen that the three occupations with the highest absenteeism were the male-dominated manual occupations followed by the female-dominated clerical workers. Unfortunately, the data is not available to consider the gender difference in absenteeism within an occupation nor the explanations for absenteeism which would be required to fully test whether absenteeism is linked with the occupation rather than the gender. The strongest conclusion possible is probably that men, on average, incur very slightly less absenteeism than women despite the male-dominated manual occupations registering relatively high rates of absenteeism.[16] However, the difference between male and female absenteeism could be distorted by the unreliable figures recorded for women in the 15–24 year age group.

Summary

For the economy's total labour force, since 1972 women have on average had shorter periods of tenure than men but, the average length of female tenure was found to have increased considerably relative to the average length of male tenure during this period. Considering the effect of occupational segregation on turnover, it was found that a substantial proportion of the gender difference in the length of tenure could be explained by segregation by occupation. With more detailed occupational blocking, the difference in tenure between men and women may be found to be considerably smaller and be linked to occupation rather than gender.

Men, on average, have marginally fewer days absent from work than do women but much of this difference in absenteeism appeared to be due to the unreliable figures for absenteeism recorded for women in the 15–24 year age bracket. It was also noted that the greatest absentee rates occurred in male-dominated (manual) occupations, suggesting that absenteeism may be linked to occupation rather than gender.

6

Trade unionism

To be a trade union member in Australia can reflect many things. It could be that the member is hoping for higher wages and/or improved working conditions, or it may simply be that the union is running a 'closed shop' which means that all employees must be union members. Although union membership does not in itself guarantee that the member will enjoy a higher wage, there have been studies undertaken that suggest that it will.[1] Trade union membership, however, may offer different advantages for men and women.

Despite there being little work undertaken on women in Australia's trade unions, a recent report[2] suggests that women have much less to gain from union membership than men.

Women are still excluded from the world of men's work and from the organisation of the paid labour force. Existence of separate unions for women historically confound arguments that women are inherently antithetical to union organisation. Many of the reasons given for lower levels of unionisation and activism also apply to men; for example, fear of discrimination, disenchantment with the operation of the union, little encouragement and absence of participatory structures. Other reasons relate specifically to women. There are many disincentives such as social factors, time, cost, especially where there are no proportional dues for part time workers, attitudes ('they don't really want us here') and few incentives for union participation by women. There is little encouragement and seldom proper recognition of women's needs...[3]

Not only do trade unions fail to establish policies to attract female employees, they also seem to actively discourage women from seeking leadership positions within the union, positions from which these women could themselves introduce policies that would benefit fellow female workers. 'Resistance to women's active participation in the union movement, in their own unions and those joint bodies that are increasingly important in relation to government policy is very strong...'[4]

Without adequate female representation on trade union policy committees, it will be unusual for trade unions to offer incentives for female membership, especially if the nature of the work undertaken by women means that the interests of women compete with those of the male employees. Nevertheless, despite this lack of female representation in trade unions the membership rates for women have increased dramatically since 1910, although this membership may be due to workplace practices and changes in the structure of the labour market rather than the advantages delivered to women by the unions.

This chapter considers three aspects of trade unionism:

1 the proportion of the male and female labour force unionised from 1910 until 1986;
2 the relationship between trade unionism and segregation by occupation;
3 the relationship between trade unionism and segregation by industry.

Male and female trade union membership

Figure 6.1[5] shows a strong increase in female trade union membership between 1910 (when only 7.5 per cent of the female labour force were unionised) and 1986 (when this figure had risen to 44.0 per cent). The proportion of the male labour force that were trade union members also increased throughout this period, from 44.4 per cent to 63.0 per cent. Men have had noticeably smaller increases in trade union membership than women in most of the years studied. Nevertheless, men have maintained a substantially higher proportion of their labour force unionised than have women. The proportion of men that are currently trade

Figure 6.1 Trade union membership, 1910–86

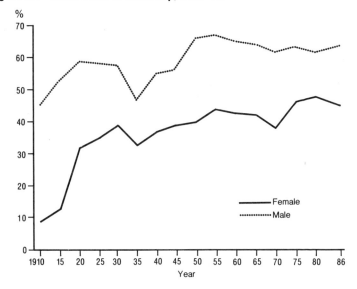

Sources: Plowman (1978 as cited by Eccles 1982), ABS (6323.0, 1984 and 1986)

union members is approximately 19 percentage points more than the female membership.

There have been two periods of substantial decrease in trade union membership for both genders since 1910. The first decrease in trade union membership occurred during the depression and pre-war years of the 1930s. The second fall in unionism occurred at the end of the boom years of the 1960s. Interestingly, male unionism never regained the high numbers it held during the 1960s, but has instead stabilised at roughly 5 per cent lower in the seventies. Women, on the other hand, increased their trade union membership throughout the early 1970s by approximately 5 per cent, stabilising at this figure in the mid-seventies[6] and incurring a slight drop in the early eighties (from 47 per cent in 1980 to 44 per cent in 1986).

Segregation and trade union membership

Women are concentrated in occupations and industries that have low levels of trade union membership.

Table 6.1   Union membership within segregated occupations, 1986

Occupation status	% of females unionised	% of males unionised
Disproportionately female (>50% female)	31.6	40.1
Well represented (20–50% female)	51.4	52.0
Disproportionately male (<20% female)	39.6	52.5
Overall	39.1	50.1

Source: ABS 6325, August 1986

Levels of unionisation are lower in small workplace industries...Two-thirds of women in New South Wales are employed in workplaces with fewer than 50 employees, and women are overrepresented in industries with a high proportion of small-workplace employment. Small workplaces are more difficult for unions to organise, particularly if there is part-time, temporary and casual employment and high turnover.[7]

Women are amongst those low-paid workers not covered by awards, such as community service workers and outworkers. Many women are also employed in small enterprises, which are difficult for unions to contact easily.[8]

Table 6.1[9] shows trade union membership within the occupational groupings provided by the ABS. Male trade unionism is highest in the male-dominated occupations and is lowest in the female-dominated occupations. This is the pattern that would be expected if men were using trade unionism to successfully exclude women from the male dominated working places. Female trade unionism follows a perverse pattern, being *lowest* in female-dominated occupations and *highest* in well represented occupations which suggests that women are not using trade unionism to exclude men from the female-dominated occupations.

Similarly, Table 6.2[10] compares trade union membership with industrial segregation. It can be seen that male trade union membership is disproportionately larger in those industries which have a disproportionately large male work force, and is smallest in the well represented industries.

Table 6.2   Union membership within segregated industries, 1986

Industry status	% of females unionised	% of males unionised
Disproportionately female (>50% female)	41.4	46.2
Well Represented (20–50% female)	37.0	44.7
Disproportionately male (<20% female)	32.3[a]	67.6
Overall	39.1	50.1

Note: [a] Liable to large statistical error
Source: ABS (6325, August 1986)

This pattern of male trade unionism is not the same for segregation by occupation, but the highest membership is once again found in the male-dominated work places. The greatest female trade unionism occurs in the female-dominated industries and the smallest occurs in the male-dominated industries.

Women show a consistent pattern of union membership within *industries* but men do not. Men show a consistent pattern of trade union membership within *occupations* but women do not. Although Australian trade unions are occupation based (rather than industry based as is often found in America), these findings do not really support the claim that men (or women) are successfully using trade unionism to exclude the other sex. Rather, it would appear that men are more likely to be trade union members and that this trend is especially strong in the male-dominated work places.

Summary

The proportion of the female labour force that were members of trade unions was found to have increased greatly, relative to male membership, since 1910. The gap between male and female trade unionism is now 19 percentage points, with men having the higher membership figures. It was also found that male trade union membership was highest in the male-dominated work places. Nonetheless, these male membership figures were not necessarily associated with the exclusion of women from occupations and industries. Rather, it appeared that the high rates of trade union membership in the male-dominated work places merely illustrated a trend for more men to be union members. Similarly, female trade unionism showed no consistent relationship between trade union membership and the exclusion of men from their working places, suggesting that female trade unionism may be influenced by other factors such as social custom and union-employer arrangements.[11]

7

Unemployment

Unemployment creates suffering and hardship for the person involved; it also represents a loss of resources to the economy, since the workplace abilities and productivity of the unemployed are wasted while unused.

The majority of data used in this chapter is taken from the Australian Bureau of Statistics (ABS). ABS statistics referring to women's unemployment are particularly vulnerable to statistical error, due to the definition of the labour force used by the ABS when collecting data. Depending on the survey type, to be included in the labour force a person must have been actively seeking work in the week or fortnight prior to the questionnaire.

A discouraged worker is someone who is willing and able to start work but is not actively seeking work because s/he believes suitable work is not available. It is often claimed that women are more easily discouraged from actively seeking work than are men.[1] In 1987 it was estimated[2] that 74.7 per cent of the discouraged workers in the market place were women.[3]

The presence of discouraged workers will bias the unemployment figures for women downward.[4] The discouraged worker effect is not constant but varies with the business cycle[5]; the extent of this bias will therefore increase during recessions, making it appear that women suffer less unemployment relative to men during economic downturns.[6]

While the discouraged worker effect should be remembered when considering the following analysis of unemployment, it will not be explicitly discussed for the rest of the chapter. Instead discussion within this chapter will first deal with the unemployment rates of men and women since 1972. The discussion then considers the last occupation (in-

Figure 7.1 Unemployed persons, August 1972–87 Proportion of the civilian workforce

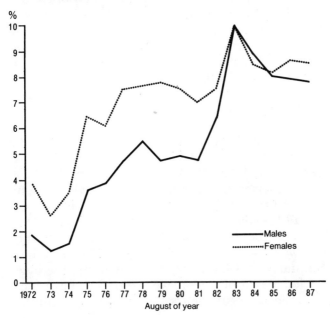

Sources: ABS (6101 1983 and 1986), ABS (6203 August 1987)

dustry) that the currently unemployed worked in according to the ABS statistics.

Figure 7.1[7] shows the unemployment rates of men and women annually since 1972. As can be seen, female unemployment was considerably greater than male unemployment throughout the seventies. In the early eighties this pattern altered. The unemployment rates for both genders peaked at a similar value in 1983 and then fell, with women actually having less unemployment than men in 1984. This fluctuation in the series may be due to the ABS changing its definitions of participation and unemployment (as was discussed with Figure 2.3). Since 1985, the pattern of the seventies seems to be re-emerging—female unemployment rate is higher than male unemployment rate and the gap between the two genders is quite substantial.

Interestingly, this difference in unemployment does not appear to be due to women lacking educational requirements.[8] Rather, 5.6 per cent of women with tertiary qualifications were unemployed while only 1.8 per cent of men with tertiary qualifications could not find work. Similarly the unemployment rate for women with a trade, technical or other certificate was 6.0 per cent, substantially higher than the 3.8 per cent of men with the same qualifications. This trend continued throughout the educational levels, only to be reversed in the group of men who did not attain the highest secondary education level. This group had a slightly higher unemployment rate of 8.3 per cent compared to 8.2 per cent for the women.

The conclusion that unemployment has been considerably higher for women than for men for twelve of the last fifteen years (excluding 1983, 1984 and 1985) is particularly disturbing considering the results we have previously found. In Chapter 5, 'Turnover and Absenteeism', women were found to have had remarkably stable *employment* rates relative to men in two of the three industries tested, while in the third industry women increased their employment relative to men. Similarly, in Chapter 2, 'Participation', the aggregate hours of female employment were found to have increased relative to the aggregate hours of male employment throughout the decade.

The apparent contradiction between the conclusions of earlier chapters (where female employment was found to be increasing relative to male employment) and the result found here (that female unemployment has not decreased relative to men throughout the same time period) may be explained in terms of relative differences in participation rates throughout the decade. To be unemployed, by definition, the person must be participating in the labour market (ie, actively seeking paid employment). Of all those people who are participating some will be successful in finding work and others will remain unemployed. The *unemployment rate* is simply the ratio of those unable to find work over all those who are participating.

If the participation rate for women greatly increased, then it is possible that the number of women employed can increase while, at the same time, the proportion of women who are unemployed can also rise. This problem will be escalated if job opportunities for women are limited. We found in Chapters 2 and 3 that women are segregated into a minority of occupations and industries. It would

Table 7.1 **Unemployment rates within segregated occupations, 1987**

Occupation status	% of females unemployed	% of males unemployed
Disproportionately female (>50% female)	4.4	4.4
Well represented (20–50% female)	3.4	5.3
Disproportionately male (<20% female)	5.8	4.9
Total for occupations	4.1	5.0
Total for the economy	8.7	7.9

Source: ABS (6203, August 1987)

appear then, that while *employment* in female-dominated occupations and industries has increased, this increase has not been as great as the gains in the participation rates for women overall. In other words, increases in the female labour force are exceeding the increases in available female jobs. If this phenomenon is occurring, the unemployment figures for women should indicate that a substantial proportion of potential workers are without recent work experience, and that this proportion would be much larger for women than for men.

Table 7.1[9] groups the unemployed according to the occupation they last worked in. The occupations are grouped into three categories; disproportionately female, well represented and disproportionately male. The criteria used when setting these categories comes from Moir and Selby-Smith.[10] If an occupation (industry for Table 7.2) had a work force consisting of more than 50 per cent women it was considered to be disproportionately female. If 20 to 50 per cent of its work force were women it was considered to be well represented, while if less than 20 per cent of the workforce were women it meant that the occupation (or industry) was included in the disproportionately male category.

Male unemployment was found to be highest in the well represented category of occupations and lowest in the female-dominated occupations. Female unemployment follows an unpredicted pattern: it was highest in the male-dominated occupations and lowest in the well represented

Table 7.2   Unemployment rates within segregated industries, 1987

Industry status	% of females unemployed	% of males unemployed
Disproportionately female (>50% female)	4.4	4.8
Well represented (20–50% female)	4.3	4.8
Disproportionately male (<20% female)	1.9[a]	6.4
Total for industries	4.2	5.2
Total for the economy	8.7	7.9

Note: [a] Liable to large statistical error
Source: ABS (6203, August 1987)

category. Men and women had the same unemployment rate of 4.4 per cent in the female-dominated occupations. What is interesting in Table 7.1 is the difference between the two total rows. The second last row of the table, 'Total for occupations', provides the total unemployment rates for women and men that have had paid employment some time within the last two years prior to being surveyed. The final row of the table, 'Total for the economy', gives the total unemployment rates for all women and men in the economy.

The difference between the two—that is, the total unemployment rates for all men and women in the economy and the unemployment rates for occupations—is due to the presence of members of the unemployed with no recent work experience. This difference is considerably larger for women (4.6 per cent) than for men (2.9 per cent), suggesting that recent increases in the female labour force have been considerably larger than recent increases in the male labour force. This result supports our earlier finding (in Chapter 2) that the growth in women's participation has exceeded increases in men's participation. It is this greater increase in female participation rates compared to female job opportunities that is creating the effect of the female unemployment rate exceeding the male unemployment rate while female employment was increasing relative to male employment.

Table 7.2[11] considers a very similar measure as Table 7.1, for *industrial* segregation. The male unemployment rate is highest in the male-dominated industries with little difference in male unemployment between the well represented and female-dominated industries. Women again provide an unpredicted result: female unemployment is slightly higher in the female-dominated industries than in the well represented category and is noticeably lower in male-dominated industries. However the estimates for female unemployment in the male-dominated industries are subject to large statistical error due to the small numbers of women involved. This has been signified by a superscript 'a' in the table. The difference between overall unemployment rates and those found within the industries is again considerably larger for women than for men (4.5 per cent for women and 2.7 per cent for men).

It is worth noting that the female-dominated occupations and industries do not stand out as having especially high unemployment rates. Rather, in Chapters 2 and 3 these occupations and industries were found to have relatively stronger growth rates in employment, providing further justification for our claim that the high rates of female unemployment noted earlier in this chapter are due to large increases in the participation rates for women rather than retrenchments of women previously employed.

Summary

Female unemployment has been considerably larger than male unemployment throughout the 1970s. Male and female unemployment showed some fluctuation in the early eighties before levelling out, with women having higher unemployment levels than men since 1984. This trend for women to have a higher unemployment rate than men has occurred despite increases in female employment relative to male employment, and does not appear to be linked with education levels. Rather, the explanation appears to be due to the large increases in the number of women entering the work force to seek paid employment. This gain in the female participation rate has far exceeded the increase in jobs available for women. Thus, while the actual number of women employed has risen, their unemployment rate has remained high.

II

Explaining the labour market

8

Orthodox theories

Orthodox models use a simple Neo-Classical economic base. In other words, they assume that the market place is typified by competition. This means that the primary motivation of employers is to make profits and that the primary motivation of workers is to maximise their life-time earnings. The implications of this framework are expanded in this chapter. Orthodox authors often rely on the use of mathematical notation to express their ideas, these equations have been included in the endnotes. An attempt has been made to fully explain the concepts within the text for readers less familiar with mathematics.

Human capital theory

Human capital is a term used to discuss the level of education skills (both general and job specific skills) that a worker has acquired. According to authors such as Becker,[1] devoting time to studying and acquiring skills is a form of investment because such work is not undertaken for its own present benefit but rather for the future pecuniary and non-pecuniary benefits it will generate. By spending resources on their education in the present period, individuals can increase their future 'time-stream of wages'.

The human capital model assumes that people have *rational* ideas of their earning and training opportunities and of their abilities. This implies that people will choose an optimal 'career path', which means that they calculate a period by period (such as year by year) combination of current earning activity and human investment activity so as to maximise their expected life time income. Furthermore, the possible costs of their investment in human capital (tuition fees, lost wages, less leisure time etc.) must be deducted from their estimated life time income.[2, 3]

The model can be considered in familiar supply and demand terms. On the demand side individuals face internal rates of return for their years of schooling. In other words, different students will have different levels of natural abilities for education; the lower the level of ability the more expensive further education becomes not only in increased tuition fees but also because more time must be expended on learning. The incentive for students to stay in school is the higher wage rate that they can receive in the labour market. On the supply side the individual is faced with the costs of the funds that they must raise to pay for their education and their living expenses while they remain at school. These costs will be affected by the interest rate the student may have to pay to acquire these funds. Even if students do not have to borrow money (if, for instance, their parents are paying for their education) they are still losing the wages they could be earning if they were employed in the labour market rather than at school. The human capital model assumes that students can calculate all of these costs and possible gains, not only for the next year, but for their entire lifetime in advance. Thus, if individuals expect to spend less time in the labour market, they will invest less in education.[4] Similarly, if individuals have lower scholastic ability they will require a greater investment to acquire a given level of training and the subsequently higher costs they face will discourage them from further training.

The human capital model concentrates on the supply side of the labour market. The demand side (how many workers employers want) is assumed to be determined in a perfectly competitive market[5] and is therefore outside the concerns of the individual decision maker. The wage that an employee receives will be equal to her marginal productivity alone which is, in turn, a function of the level of investment in human capital that the individual has incurred. The individual chooses her level of investment rationally with full knowledge of her abilities and labour market duration. Parents investing on the behalf of children will make similar rational decisions.[6]

To reiterate, if an individual invests relatively less in

training then, according to the human capital theory, this will be due to the individual either:

1 having lower scholastic ability;
2 expecting to spend less time in the labour market;
3 being unduly affected in their propensity to invest by outside cultural and institutional factors (for instance, cultural attitudes that dictate that women should not work in the traditional labour market). It is assumed that all individuals of equal investment levels will receive equal wages in the perfectly competitive labour market.

The proposition that on average women receive lower wages within the labour market than do men is therefore answered by followers of the human capital model within these terms. An excellent example is provided by Mincer.[7] Mincer's analysis contains the main elements of the human capital model explained so far. However, Mincer provides an explicit justification for women investing relatively smaller sums in market-related training schemes than men, that is, he poses an alternative to market work for women: non-market labour (or, as it is more commonly known, housework).

According to Mincer there is no simple choice between market labour, valued in exchange terms, and leisure. Rather, the analyst needs to consider the presence of non-market work, where non-market work includes the production of commodities for the family's use and various forms of investment in the non-market worker.[8] The basic unit of analysis has now shifted from being the individual decision maker to become a family unit whose members pool their abilities in order to simultaneously maximise their own and the family's utility.[9] The family, as a whole, has a positive demand for the 'household goods and services' that non-market labour produces. This demand needs to be considered when the family is allocating its time between market work, non-market work and leisure. It is assumed that the rational combination for the family will occur when those with comparative advantages in non-market work perform these household tasks for those with a comparative advantage in market work and vice versa. In this manner the family, as a whole, can maximise its income in terms of total goods and services and simultaneously maximise the available leisure time to family members.[10]

The major difference between Mincer's analysis and that presented above is that, where other studies have discussed individuals with comparative advantages in non-market work or in market work, Mincer has discussed wives and husbands respectively. If the constraints are valid, then Mincer's analysis claims that as a husband's income increases his wife will consume more leisure with subsequently less market and non-market work. Yet simultaneously, if the wife's income from market sources increases she will not consume more leisure but will rather engage in more market work.[11]

Mincer's analysis raises the fundamental issue of why it is assumed that women have comparative advantages in non-market, household skills. Mincer seems to have been influenced by Becker when making this assumption.

Becker[12] appears to take an undefined stance on the basis of his assumption that women have a comparative advantage for non-market work, or equivalently, that they have a comparative disadvantage for market work. On the one hand, Becker argues that the genders have 'basic biological differences' which are the source of systematic differences in the capabilities of men and women. He argues that these biological differences lead to a home-oriented allocation of time and thus composition of human capital for women. This is reflected in lower market wages for women and, in turn, further reinforces the home role of women.[13] Economic pressures will therefore reinforce the behavioural outcomes of the original biological differences.

However, in Chapter 7 of the same book, Becker starts the causal chain from the other end. Higher market wages for women, he argues, will change female allocations, the composition of women's human capital and even the division of non-market work within the family. Thus, it would appear that sex roles are responsive to market forces.

When the analyst is faced with a situation of relatively low market wages and low market participation rates for women, two logical conclusions flow from Becker's theory. First, high levels of natural ability for household tasks have led women to incur low levels of investment in human capital which, in turn, has led to their low market wages. Or second, (an equally logical conclusion), the low market wages have led women to expect low rates of return for their investments in human capital thus encouraging them to spend more time at home developing household skills. To test whether women have higher natural abilities for household tasks or whether they have actually acquired these skills during their lifetimes would seem to be an impossibility and, in fact, Becker's model is very difficult to test empirically.[14] This appears to leave Becker's theory in a weak position where it may be of little use to the analyst.

The human capital theorists generally assume that labour markets operate perfectly. Therefore, any wage difference between the genders can only be due to different levels of investment in human capital, ruling out the possibility of women specialising in home tasks because they receive relatively inequitable wages.

Given the doubts and difficulties associated with the human capital theories, the predictions arising from these models can nevertheless be considered in terms of our earlier findings. Specifically the models predict a similar wage level for workers of similar education levels regardless of gender. We found in Chapters 3 and 4 that this was not the case. Rather, it appeared that women with high education levels were nevertheless employed in low paying occupations and industries. The human capital models also predict that, on average, men have less turnover and higher levels of investment in market orientated training than do women. The results of Chapter 5 support this prediction (women were found to have lower tenure rates than men) but the strong implication of Chapter 5 was that the major explanation for women having lower tenure rates was the occupations in which women were concentrated. It would appear that the human capital model is not providing a satisfactory explanation of the position of women in the Australian labour market.

Taste theory

Becker's assumption of a perfectly competitive labour market does not mean that he excluded the possibility of discrimination within the labour force. Rather, he seemed to be very aware of the effect of such practices.[15] One of the many models Becker constructed that could cope with the presence of discrimination was the 'taste for discrimination' theory. In this model Becker drew an analogy between discrimination and the other broad range of tastes and preferences underlying an individual's labour market choices. Thus, just as an employee might prefer to work in an outdoor environment, he might prefer not to work with women.

Given the assumption that all people want to maximise their level of happiness or satisfaction,[16] then these *tastes* in combination with relative prices will determine the individual's market behaviour.

Discrimination is not without cost; discrimination that leads to either wage or employment differentials between groups discourages workers from the disadvantaged group from seeking work. The employer who practices discrimination will be faced with an inferior workforce. The subsequent loss of efficiency leads to increased costs for firms, employers will attempt to pass these costs on to the group which has the taste for discrimination in the form of lower wages. If male employees do not want to work with women, then the men must pay for this taste for discrimination by receiving lower wages. A wage or employment differential can occur between men and women performing the same tasks in different locations, if men (women) have a distaste for working alongside or associating with women (men), and if men (women) are prepared to pay for having their tastes satisfied by receiving lower wages than they would otherwise receive.

Becker considers the taste for discrimination to be caused by attitudes within the society rather than the individual. This begs the question as to where such discrimination begins and, by implication, would lead us into a similar circular argument explaining female participation as was presented in the human capital theory. Becker also ignores the possibility of discrimination being supply side orientated, thus assuming that the employer cannot be an active discriminator. Becker's assumption of a perfectly competitive labour market may be unrealistic in a highly regulated country such as Australia, where there is much opportunity for employers to discriminate. Arrow[17] highlights another difficulty with Becker's model, for unless the discrimination is uniformly spread across the economy the disadvantaged group can seek work with the less discriminatory employers and begin to push their wage up. Akerlof provides possible justification for these practices being widespread by claiming that customers 'will boycott any firm that violates a discriminatory social custom'.[18]

An interesting empirical implication of the taste theory is that men working in a male concentrated environment will be receiving lower wages than those men who are not displaying discriminatory tastes and are working with women. We found in Chapters 3 and 4 that the industries and occupations that have high concentrations of male employees do not receive lower wages. Instead, these workplaces typically received relatively higher wages, suggesting that the taste for discrimination model finds it difficult to account for the more obvious characteristics of the Australian labour market.

Search theory

Search theory may be used as an explanation for those unemployment differentials between the sexes that might otherwise be credited to discrimination. Search theory accepts that markets are not typified by perfect knowledge in the real world. Authors such as Stigler[19] remind us that gathering information about the variety of job opportunities and wage offers involves the individual in costly searches. The cost of these searches increases with the length of time the search proceeds and the spatial region the searcher must cover. The potential returns to the search increase with higher wages and expected length of tenure in the new job. Periods of frictional unemployment, during which people seek out their best work alternatives, are then part of optimising behavioural patterns.

Search theories are often based on the human capital model, with the underlying assumptions already discussed, in particular the assumption that *women have a comparative advantage for household tasks* which, via lower investments in training, results in women receiving lower market wages and spending shorter periods in the labour market than do men. Both of these factors will decrease the potential return for women engaging in lengthy searches. Similarly, women will be hesitant to travel far from their home base where their non-market work is highly valued. They are therefore spatially limited. While this can decrease the costs of the search it also limits opportunities for women, tending to further shorten their search period. Thus, the analysis suggests that, within the orthodox framework, women would be expected to engage in shorter search periods and incur shorter periods of frictional unemployment than do men. Yet, authors such as Chirinko[20] imply that women face longer periods of frictional unemployment. The explanation for this contradiction seemingly lies with the latter author's claims that women have higher turnover rates. This claim is not necessarily derived from the behavioural assertions of the orthodox model, which instead claims that women will have a shorter total working life than will men. However, it is a natural flow on from Mincer's conclusion that women will move into and out of the labour market in response to changes in their husband's income[21]: implying that women will seek work to boost family incomes and retire when the husband's income rises.

If women have higher turnover rates than men, women would have to undertake more search periods than men. While individual search periods for women may be shorter than those for men, in total they may lead to women facing longer overall periods of frictional unemployment.

The turnover rates for men and women were studied in Chapter 5, 'Turnover and absenteeism', where it was found that women do have slightly higher turnover rates (although this appeared to be linked to occupation rather than gender). However, the results of Chapter 3 revealed that the educational levels of women had little influence on the occupations and industries that women were employed in. The highly concentrated female workplaces have, on average, considerably better qualified female than male employees. This latter result presents difficulties for the search model since the underlying explanation for women spending less time seeking jobs is because women lack investment in human capital. If women do not want to spend time in the work force why do they engage in the *irrational* accumulation of this education? It would appear then that the search model does not provide an adequate description of the participation of women in the Australian labour market.

Screening

Screening occurs when an employer uses an easily disting-
uishable characteristic of a job applicant (sex, colour etc.) as
a proxy for the expected quality of the job applicant's work.
Screening techniques (which are also known as statistical
discrimination) are argued to be a 'natural' consequence of
imperfections in the labour market due to scarcity of information regarding the existence and characteristics of
workers and jobs. Employers, in such circumstances, do not
have the resources to test each applicant fully. They therefore rely on previous statistical experience with members
of the applicant's group which they use as a weight when
considering each job applicant.[22]

Screening theories suggest that the employer uses quite
complex techniques when considering job applicants.[23]
While it is unlikely that employers carry out these steps
explicitly, it might be that employers carry out a weighting
process implicitly, in which case the weights need to be
considered in more detail. Here the theories leave us in
doubt. There are two main possibilities; the first most commonly discussed by the orthodox theorists, the second excluded as being determined independently to the market
and somehow outside the realms of economic analysis. Each
of these possibilities will be considered in turn.

Orthodox theorists discuss profit maximising firms operating in a market which suffers an imperfection because of
lack of information concerning job applicants, but is otherwise operating in a fully competitive manner. When establishing the weights to apply as proxies, such employers are
only concerned with efficiency and so will attempt to find
the least biased predictor of a group's expected work performance. If an employer has estimated accurately then, at
best, the weighting process will discriminate against members of a group who do not share their group's common
working characteristics. It is argued that in total this form
of discrimination is economically rational,[24] since the employer is crediting to the group those characteristics which
the group does, on the average, hold. (It should be noted
that economically rational discrimination for the employer
can create great hardship for those individuals who don't
share the group's characteristics but are still discriminated

against.) According to the screening model, the best cure for statistical discrimination would be to improve the working characteristics of this group.

However, if the employer has made an incorrect estimate, as is highly likely in a market characterised by imperfect information, then discrimination would occur against the group as a whole. Australian studies of tenure suggest that employers using raw data on quit rates would in fact over-estimate the quit rates of women relative to men.[25] The best solution prescribed by the screening model for this second form of discrimination is not anti-discrimination laws but, rather, providing the employer with better information concerning the group's characteristics. This issue will be discussed further in Chapter 11, 'Legislation and affirmative action'.

The second main type of weighting an employer can use for decision making is obviously a biased predictor. In other words, an estimator which systematically reflects the employer's own discrimination against a group. While such an estimator is not rational for a profit-maximising employer operating in a competitive market environment, it may readily occur in markets with limited competition.[26] In fact, in Chapter 5 employers were found to consistently under-estimate the tenure rates of women. Providing employers with better information will not remove this discrimination. Rather, it may be necessary to force the employer to cease discriminating by increasing the competition the employer faces in the labour market (removing market power and/or government protection) or by introducing anti-discrimination legislation (such as that discussed in Chapter 11).

While the screening model appears to explain the behaviour of some employers, the underlying assumptions of the model may be dubious. It was argued that women, as a group, have inferior working characteristics to men and that it was therefore rational for employers to reject women applicants. Yet, as previously discussed in this chapter (see also Chapter 12, 'Conclusion'), women do not appear to have these obviously inferior working characteristics. It was shown in Chapter 3 that once allowance was made for gender based differences in education, experience, trade union membership, country of birth, regional location, industry or occupation and marital status, the female wage was, on average, still 13 per cent lower than the average male wage. This finding indicates that the screening model cannot provide a full explanation of this Australian labour market phenomenon.

9

Institutional theories

A common feature of the orthodox models of analysis is the assumption that competitive market operations will effectively prevent the employer from engaging in any form of discrimination that is not specifically profit maximising. These orthodox models view the labour market as a giant bourse-like system, which operates to ensure full competition between all market members and, in the process, totally constrains the idiosyncratic views of particular members.

In contrast,[1] a common feature of the institutional models is the assumption that the employer possesses a degree of market power and uses it discriminately. This market power arises from the presence of multiple labour markets, each of which faces only limited competition from the other such markets.

The concept of non-competing groups within a market is not new, rather, it was already being discussed by Cairnes and Mills in the late nineteenth century.[2] This concept was adopted by Clark Kerr,[3] who discussed labour markets as being bounded by geographical, occupational and, especially, institutional factors. According to Kerr, these boundaries will touch and overlap at points but labour mobility between any two markets is highly limited. He argued that the economy is split into structured and unstructured markets. The unstructured markets are characterised by a lack of attachment between workers and the employer, except for the wage agreement. The structured market sector is again split into internal and external markets. The internal market operates as an administrative unit, shielded from the usual competitive market forces, it is characterised by a set of institutional rules which fully define the working conditions of those workers employed within this sector. The external sector is made up of would-be employees of the internal sector, who cluster around the limited ports of entry into the latter market.

Kerr's description of the labour market as being divided into small, hostile groups was further developed by authors, such as Piore and Doeringer,[4] who were attempting to explain the difficulties the civil rights movement, and President Johnson's War on Poverty campaign, were having in improving the living conditions of minority groups in America. Doeringer and Piore carried out extensive research based on relatively open ended, unstructured interviews with economic actors. They aimed at compiling a comprehensive description of the labour market as it is in reality, rather than a rigorous theoretical analysis of what form it could take given certain behavioural assertions.[5]

They concluded that the labour market consists of two main sectors, which they labelled primary and secondary. The primary sector consists of large firms all displaying a degree of market power. Employees in this sector enjoy relatively high quality working conditions; including high wages, stable employment, established promotion opportunities and participation in establishing the administrative rules governing their work environment.

The secondary sector generally consists of small peripheral firms that typically perform lowly skilled work tasks and are constantly threatened by potential competitors and/or downturns in economic activity. Workers in these firms face unattractive work packages with low wages, unstable employment, little chance of promotion and arbitrary managerial decision making. The tasks these workers carry out tend to be unskilled, monotonous and alienating. Thus, a normal working day for these secondary sector employees is unrewarding, creating a situation where employees will develop higher rates of absenteeism, turnover and generally unsatisfactory work behaviour. These unsatisfactory working patterns that secondary sector employees develop will further limit their chances of being accepted into the primary market. This exclusion greatly increases the social costs involved in such a market structure.

Access to the primary sector occurs at a limited number of 'ports of entry' which tend to be located at low level job placement. Suitable applicants enter these ports young and then progress up a promotion ladder within the large firm. Each firm uses a unique range of machinery and techniques so that the skills acquired by a worker in one firm will be irrelevant in another firm. Highly structured promotion ladders are a necessary requirement because of this firm-specific technology used in the primary sector. These ladders provide security of employment and progression for employees who accumulate large quantities of firm specific training during their working lives and are required by the employer to pass this knowledge on to newcomers via on-the-job-training techniques. Job offers are only made at very low (or very high) salary levels, limiting the movement of workers between firms and increasing the security of the promotion ladders.

This dual labour market approach therefore relies on four related hypotheses:

1   It is useful to divide the economy into a primary and a secondary sector;
2   Wages, and working conditions, will be determined by different factors in the two sectors,
3   Labour mobility between the two sectors will be highly limited,
4   The secondary sector is marked by poor working conditions and high levels of unemployment.[6]

To reiterate, the dualist approach describes the effects of institutional arrangements on the labour market. It is essentially a structural framework which can be used to highlight market difficulties but it provides no complete explanation of the development of the institutions or how they will change over time. In other words, the framework lacks a theory. Within the next two chapters institutional frameworks shall be found to have been used by authors from many philosophical backgrounds to highlight different causal relationships and behavioural assertions and often to reach contradictory conclusions.

Intra-firm segmentation

The intra-firm segmentation model is a consistent development of the dualist model. Like the dualist model it attempts to describe the labour market in a realistic manner and only then to seek a theory which can explain these findings.

Authors, such as Osterman,[7] point out that the vast majority of research into models of institutional labour market structures have been concerned with the secondary sector. In contrast, the primary sector has tended to be treated as a monolithic quantity and considered to be adequately characterised by the stylised facts presented by Doeringer and Piore in the early 1970s.[8] Osterman claims that firms, apparently operating within the primary sector, will contain separate internal market structures. Some of these internal market structures can be readily characterised as offering employment typical of the secondary sector market.[9] The essential unit for dual labour market analysis should therefore be the components of the firm rather than the firm itself.

Within a single firm, it is argued, there will typically exist three sub-systems; the industrial, the craft and the secondary sub-systems. The rules of the industrial sub-system cover managers and officials within the firm as well as technicians and some blue collar workers. The industrial sub-system involves a large quantity of firm-specific on-the-job training and limited ports of entry, at any level above base junior, making both inter and intra-firm mobility difficult. The craft sub-system contains many professional and highly skilled consultants. These workers tend to have high levels of general education; they enjoy high inter-firm mobility and are typically more loyal to their professional bodies than they are to the firm. The essential difference between the industrial and the craft sub-systems is not one of skill or wage levels (since managers etc. are included in the industrial sub-system). Rather, the distinction lies in the different set of industrial rules they face, providing them with different promotion, mobility and loyalty outcomes.

Finally, workers in the secondary sub-system tend to lack any clear advancement path, either inter or intra-firm. This creates little hope of developing a career within the sub-system. Secondary sub-system workers tend to be unskilled, lowly paid and unsatisfied. The sub-section generally contains work tasks such as clerical occupations, mail room staff, telephonists, messengers and cleaners; tasks which are typically carried out by women.

The poor working conditions of this secondary sub-system occur because firms prefer a flexible work force. In fact, Osterman argues that the firm would similarly like to break up the high cost industrial sub-system by removing much of the rigidity forced upon the firm by these employees and the lesser pressures for such structures from current technology.[10] Thus, Osterman claims that unemployment rates show a significant trend for increasing insecurity in the industrial sub-system as previously skilled jobs are automated and allocated to the deskilled secondary sub-system. The firm appears to be constantly breaking the industrial sub-system down while building up the secondary sub-system. This trend shall be considered further in the next chapter.

Osterman's analysis is valuable for emphasising the work tasks that women carry out in those industries, firms, and even occupations, that mainstream analysts may have labelled as primary labour markets. In Chapters 2–7 consideration was given to the position of women within industries, occupations and the public service to try to determine whether or not women are concentrated into the lowest skilled, poorly paid, secondary sector tasks within these institutions. Chapter 3 showed that women are concentrated into a minority of occupations and that these occupations offer lower wages. Chapter 4 revealed that women receive very little promotion in the private or public sectors. These results support the model of intra-firm segmentation. However, before the model can be fully accepted, promotion ladders within specific firms need to be studied. Unfortunately, there does not appear to be a suitable source of Australian data available for this testing.

Market efficiency

The human capital model has readily transformed itself to accommodate the dual and intra-firm labour market models. Human capital theorists explain internal market systems as structures which are necessary to cope with the firm specific nature of technology.[11] Thus, technology creates work tasks that are idiosyncratic to a particular firm. The resulting heterogeneity of jobs makes employees poor substitutes for each other, leading to low levels of inter-firm labour mobility and effectively preventing competitive market forces from establishing the wage and working conditions for these jobs.

As was discussed in the section, 'Human capital', people are willing to incur temporary losses in income to accumulate investments in human capital when they expect their future pecuniary and non-pecuniary benefit flows, so derived, to offset this initial outlay. Firm specific training, as opposed to general training, only increases the productivity of a worker in her present place of employment. Thus, the wage rate other firms offer a worker will not increase as a result of specific capital formation. The employee's willingness to incur costs in specific training will, therefore, not only depend on their expected improvements in wage and working conditions with their present employer, but also with their expected length of tenure with that employer.[12]

Standard human capital analysis[13] claims that workers receive lower wages in specific training periods than that offered by alternative sources of employment. Nevertheless, the wage rate they receive will be higher than their productivity during this training period. In the post-training period the worker will receive a wage which fully compensates for this temporary loss in income and is simultaneously higher than the wage being offered in other firms. In this way the employer and employee share the costs of specific training.

However, this analysis understates the insecurity employees may feel when considering the expense and effort required by training. Similarly, employers will be greatly affected by the expected tenure of applicants for jobs which involve the firm in costly periods of specific training. The employment and promotion structure within the firm can provide security for both parties; for employees it guarantees long term employment and promotion which is often based on seniority; for employers it enables junior base level recruitment and incremental training of workers so that, by the time expensive periods of specific training are required, the employer will be familiar with the employee's working habits and commitment. Internal labour markets thereby diminish the risk involved in specific training for both parties, enabling the market to operate more efficiently.

Discrimination does not fit easily into the model of market efficiency. According to this model of market efficiency, employers are using the internal labour market structure merely to sort out suitable long term employees. The reasons why women do not appear in the middle to higher ranges of these labour markets can be diverse. Seemingly, the most obvious would be if women have higher turnover rates than men. The data was checked for this in Chapter 5, 'Turnover and absenteeism', where it was found that women did have shorter tenure periods than men but this difference appeared to be linked with the occupations women were concentrated in rather than a gender based difference in tenure rates. Reasons for women not appearing in the lower rungs of the labour markets are more difficult to find, assuming of course that women are applying for entrance. Scarcity of women in these positions can only be explained by statistical, or other forms of, discrimination being used in the employment decisions which effectively screen women out. Chapter 4 suggests that a significant proportion of the different treatment of men and women by employers is not due to dissimilar working characteristics between the sexes. This conclusion contradicts the commonly-made assumption in economic theory that employers will compete with each other to minimise costs. An employer who will discriminate against a *productive* employee because of sex will end up paying higher wages for a less productive work force. This is not competitive behaviour, nor is it efficient, suggesting that the model of market efficiency (with its intra-firm segmentation) does not provide an adequate description of the Australian labour market.

Monopsonistic competition

The following discussion provides a simplified explanation of this complicated economic model.[14]

The term *monopsonist* means single buyer. If an employee faces a monopsonistic employer then this means that that worker can only be employed by that employer. Monopsonists have great power over potential workers; they can deny job opportunities and set all working conditions. For instance, in Australia there are no private armies: this means that if a worker wants to be a soldier then s/he can only be employed by the Defence Forces. If s/he is accepted, the Defence Force sets all wage and working conditions.

The term *monopsonistic competition* has a broader definition. Monopsonistic competition occurs when there are many buyers (in our case the employers) who have a powerful labour market position. They distinguish between potential employees and treat different groups of employees dissimilarly. These employers have the *power* to deny job opportunities and to set working conditions as might a 'pure' monopsonist.

It will be in the interests of monopsonistic employers to discriminate against those minority groups that lack market power. By reducing the wages of minority groups the employer can reduce the total wage bill. Monopsonistic employers may also mistakenly believe that some groups of workers are more productive than others. This can become a self-fulfilling prophecy if the favoured group have increased opportunities and training. If employers differentiate between men and women, by treating men as superior workers to women, women would have less sources of employment than men.

An effective means of dealing with this segregation (short of removing the monopsonists themselves) is to remove the basis for discrimination against female employees, either by improving the productivity of female employees, by increasing the market power of women or, if the segregation is unfounded on efficiency grounds, rendering illegal such discrimination.[15]

Although it is often difficult to directly measure market power, trade union membership may be used as an indicator. The findings of Chapter 6 showed that women have greatly increased their levels of trade union membership throughout this century but very few women are found in policy forming positions in these trade unions and it does not appear that unions are fully supporting the wants of female members. Market power can be increased by *decreasing* the number of women seeking work in a particular occupation: the less competition each applicant faces the stronger will be her bargaining position. The results of Chapter 3 show that women are concentrated into a minority of occupations and that the types of occupations offering women employment have undergone little change since 1911.

Women face large levels of competition from fellow female employees resulting in their having low levels of market power.

Chapters 3 and 4 considered the effects of equal pay legislation on female wages and employment levels in an attempt to ascertain whether or not women face monopsonistic employers. The introduction of equal pay legislation led to roughly 20 per cent higher wages for women and yet this wage rise did not result in a fall in the employment rate of women. On the contrary, their employment figures rose.

Consideration was also given to female segmentation and the more obvious measures of efficiency (general education, turnover, absenteeism etc.) in an attempt to discover whether or not discrimination against women is based on efficiency grounds. The strong conclusion of Chapter 4 was that even after allowing for differences in working characteristics, there was substantial difference in the treatment of men and women by employers. These results support the claims of the monopsonistic competition model: women do appear to be facing a limited number of employers who have sufficient market power to discriminate against them.

Overcrowding

It is possible for workers to increase their wages by forcing other workers out of their labour market. For instance, if male employees can ensure that no women can compete against them for jobs in a certain occupation (by forming agreements with employers that exclude women), then these men can expect to receive a higher wage because:

1 employers will have fewer workers to choose from and will therefore need to pay higher wages to attract scarce workers away from competitors;
2 there will be fewer workers in any particular workplace so the relative productivity of each worker will rise.

Having been denied an opportunity to work in the male dominated (preferred) occupation, women must seek work elsewhere and thereby become crowded into a narrow range of occupations. The high unemployment rate among women will lead them to compete against each other for the available jobs and will thereby push the wage rate down. As so many women have been crowded into these female-dominated occupations, there should always be a considerable amount of female unemployment which will hold this wage down. Employers will respond to the lower wage by taking on more women which will decrease the relative productivity of the female workers until their productivity equals the lower wage. Thus, we have a scenario whereby an original discriminatory act by men can lead to different wage levels between men and women, as well as correspondingly different productivity levels across the sexes. This is a common example of the use of market power and it is often argued that male trade unions attempt to bring about this situation.

There is, however, a major obstacle to the success of the trade union's policy. It is in the interest of the employers in the male preferred occupation to seek out female workers to break the male stranglehold on supply and lead to a fall in the male wage rate. Trade unions need to form 'sweetheart' deals with employers to prevent this from happening but this arrangement will be insecure from the union point of view and less than optimal for the employers.

This is the traditional Overcrowding model.[16] Bergmann adapts this model by considering the situation in which it will be in the employers' interest to have women discriminated against. Employers typically will not employ only one occupational category of workers, rather they will employ from managers through to cleaners. If the wage rate of women is held down in the menial worktasks this can decrease the total wage bill for the employer, depending on what proportion of the work force is female and how responsive male and female workers are to varying wage rates. In this situation there will be no tension between the employers and the discriminatory male trade unions, instead the discrimination against women may become an easy to police gentlemen's agreement across employers.[17]

The extent of occupational segregation in the labour market, and its effect on female wages and unemployment,[18] was considered earlier in this study to try to ascertain whether or not the indirect evidence supports Bergmann's conclusion. It was found in Chapters 3 and 4 that women are segregated into a minority of occupations, and that these occupations were typified by low wage levels and

were generally considered as menial. Furthermore, despite
dramatic increases in the participation rates of women (see
Chapter 2) the occupational segregation of women has
shown negligible change since 1911. Chapter 7 revealed that
women endure higher unemployment rates than men but
the unemployment rates for women are highest for those
women seeking work in the male-dominated occupations,
not in the female-dominated industries. This contradicts the
predictions of the overcrowding models, suggesting that the
models do not *fully* explain the dynamics of the Australian
labour market.

Regional segmentation

Working within the internal labour market structure, Francine Blau[19] argues that employers face little freedom in
establishing wage or working conditions. Instead, the employer is faced with a very extensive set of institutional
constraints (such as Arbitration Commission rulings) which
includes a rigid wage structure specifying the wage relativities between occupational categories and types of
employees.[20]

Within any particular geographical region, some industries will be successful and profitable, others will operate
closer to the edge and will be more vulnerable to the booms
and recessions of the business cycle. Blau argues that employers in the secure and profitable industries will discriminate against female employees simply because they can
afford the luxury of inefficient discrimination. This means
that women must seek work in the riskier industries that
offer lower wages, less satisfactory working conditions and
the constant possibility of retrenchment.

According to this model high profit industries will offer
relatively high wages and will employ a disproportionately
large male work force. This conclusion is the opposite of
that prescribed by Becker's taste theory[21] (Chapter 8) where
men must pay for the privilege of having their taste for
discrimination satisfied.

The findings in Chapters 3 and 4 support Blau's claim
that the male-dominated industries have higher wages but
these industries were not found to be the most secure and

profitable industries to work in. Rather, Chapter 2 indicates that the male-dominated industries (and occupations) typically had the smallest growth rates and the highest retrenchment figures. This finding totally contradicts the explanation provided by the regional segmentation model.

10

Radical theories

The radical models considered in this chapter are based on a Marxian economic framework.[1] In simple terms, Marxists claim the labour market can be split between those who own the tools and equipment necessary for production (the capitalists) and those who must work for the capitalists. The capitalists will pay the workers as little as possible regardless of how productive the workers are. Furthermore, the Marxian framework predicts how the labour market will change over time. It is claimed that the *number* of capitalists will decrease but that those capitalists left will accumulate greater stocks of machinery and tools (capital) which they will use to replace workers in the production process. This will lead to greater unemployment and suffering amongst the workers (the proletariat). It will also lead to increasingly severe business cycles (booms and recessions) until, eventually, the working class will rise up and overthrow the capitalists.

The Marxian model is exceedingly more intricate and sophisticated than this introduction would suggest. Every attempt has been made throughout this chapter to present the radical models in an understandable form without removing the gist of the arguments.

Segmented labour markets

The segmented labour market model adopts the basic institutional framework and extends it out by placing it within an historical context and a Marxian theory. Hence, Reich, Gordon and Edwards[2] argue that the diverse market structures of the institutionalist models are merely a characteristic of the present historical period of segmentation which, in turn, is a stage in the process of capital accumulation.

The segmented model considers three distinct historical phases generated by the process of capital accumulation. Each epoch is characterised by the form of labour organisation that occurs within it. The form of labour organisation is assumed to be determined by the capitalist class as they attempt to control and exploit the working class. After the establishment of a new phase of capital accumulation, with its accompanying mode of labour organisation, there will be a lengthy period of economic prosperity and stability. Inevitably, however, the economy will enter a series of cyclical swings between boom and recession. These swings will be of increasing severity and the epoch will enter into a decay period. Associated with these economic cycles is increasing discontent and political uprising by the workers. Eventually the capitalists will be forced to devise a new form of labour organisation, which fully considers the current form and base of the workers' political power, and there will be a transformation to a new epoch where the process will begin again.[3]

The third, and current, epoch is called the stage of capital accumulation. During this stage it is argued that the capitalists explicitly recognised the potential revolutionary threat of the unified workers, responding to this threat by devising a form of labour market organisation which aimed at dividing the labour force.[4] First, the capitalists deliberately devised the structure of internal labour markets (see Chapter 9) with its obvious hierarchical arrangement.[5] Within large firms, many of these internal market structures were developed, each with different ports of entry and different possible promotion outcomes. This enabled the employer to further segment workers according to their education levels, social background, racial or sexual characteristics by allocating each group to a different job ladder with different wage levels, promotion possibilities and social status.[6] These differences in the obvious characteristics of employees (such as being male or female) are further exploited by the monopolists by using a group as strike breakers or as wage undercutters.[7] This situation ensures that the working class will not unite.

As the monopolistic corporations fought to increase their

market control, they rejected those markets which were typified by fluctuating demands or unreliable sources. This left the unreliable and inherently unprofitable markets to small periphery firms, these markets are the highly competitive, high risk, low satisfaction sector which Piore[8] described as the secondary sector.[9] By refusing to employ an ex-employee of the secondary sector, monopsonists ensure that there will be limited common experiences and relationships between primary and secondary workers.

The segmented theory does appear to provide a valid description of the labour market which has developed in the postwar period, although it can be criticised[10] as merely attempting to rationalise the current labour market structure of America. According to the discussion of the segmentationist theory, three main types of segmentation would be expected to occur within the labour market:

1 Segmentation into primary and secondary markets as the monopolists reject those markets typified by cyclical demand and uncertainty.
2 Segmentation within the primary sector, with the development of numerous different employment and promotion ladders.
3 Segmentation by sex, race, and obvious social characteristics whereby members of minority groups are denied entry to optimal job ladders and are only offered jobs which are typically servile in nature, have inferior promotion prospects and working conditions and/or are located in the secondary labour market.

According to the segmentation theory, the cure for sexual discrimination is not to increase the productivity of women or to provide greater information flows to employers. Segmentation theory claims that discrimination is a deliberate act on behalf of employers to limit labour power and has absolutely no relevance to the productivity of the workers involved. The cure for such discrimination is to remove the capitalist's power directly by removing the means of production and, thus, their right to employ, or indirectly by enforcing legislation which will make such employment patterns illegal, thereby forcing the capitalists to devise a new method of labour organisation which does not rely on discrimination.

It is difficult to devise empirical tests for the segmentation theory which are different to those applied to the institutionalist model. In its description of the segmentation epoch the segmentation model combines many of the aspects considered in Chapter 9, for instance, inter and intra-firm discrimination and overcrowding of groups into limited job ladders, a primary and secondary sector etc. However, there does appear to be at least one significant testable prediction generated by the segmentationist model that differs to the combined institutionalist approach. According to Reich,[11] the process of segmentation has developed greatly since the Second World War as the epoch of segmentation developed and entered into its decay stage in the 1970s. Hence, there should be a noticeable difference in segmentation in the pre and post Second World War periods and the extent of segregation should be increasing in the post war period. In Chapter 3, however, it was found that the *number* of women working in the disproportionately female occupations rose but the number of women working in male-dominated occupations also rose. The *proportion* of the female workforce found in the female-dominated occupations remained remarkably stable, around 80 per cent between 1911 and 1985. This finding does not support the predictions of the model of segmented labour markets, suggesting that we should not accept the model as an adequate description of the Australian labour market.

Neo-Marxists

There are a vast number of neo-Marxist theories, many of which hold different models of labour market development and the role of women within it.[12] Only two shall be considered here, and the second only briefly.

In general, neo-Marxists separate the capitalist period into two phases. In the first phase industrialists sought to replace the general skills of the craftsman/peasant farmer with job specific skills more suitable for the specialised work in industry. In the second phase capitalists used technology and scientific management to deliberately deskill workers, decreasing mental labour from their work and creating a constantly increasing proportion of alienating occupations. Each new phase of capitalist expansion displaces labour from previously satisfying jobs and creates new supplies of labour for these inferior occupations. Thus, as capitalism expanded into domestic production, women were forced out of the household and onto the labour market, where they took up employment in these alienating work tasks. This trend for the proportion of secondary market jobs to grow relative to previously skilled and satisfying jobs reflects the constantly increasing suffering of the working class which is supposedly associated with the second phase capitalist period.

Within the neo-Marxist models, internal labour markets and occupational stratifications are merely artificial devices used by employers to gain control over workers, and work standards, in order to exploit and control workers (by segmenting workers and promoting employee identification with goals of the firm). Therefore, the neo-Marxists initially appear to have much in common with the segmentationists discussed in the previous section. (Indeed, many of the segmentationists claim to be neo-Marxists). However, whereas the segmentationists focus on transformations between different epochs within the period of capital accumulation, the neo-Marxists see the capitalist period as one of increasing suffering of the proletariat. This single capitalist period is essentially continuous, although it will encounter fluctuations when the economy enters its inevitable cyclical swings.[13]

Humphries explicitly considers the role of women in the family and in the labour force within a neo-Marxist framework.[14] For Humphries the family is defended by the working class who see it as an obstacle to the cheapening of labour. The working class defence of its standard of living depends on it maintaining a given real wage level and also the domestic production of valuables. Maintaining the family structure aids both of these defences and male opposition to female employment is therefore not seen as being generated by self interest, but rather, by their desire to remove females from competing with them in the labour market in order to maximise the family's real income. The essence of this action is that it constitutes class action, women are members of the classes. While the class action to bid up the price of labour may have caused great hardship to individual working class women, it has improved the living standards of working class women as a whole and is therefore justifiable in a neo-Marxist context. An unfortunate side effect of this is the commonly expressed view that women belong in the home, especially married women. This has reinforced the sex-based relations of dominance and subordination already practised in the community.[15]

Humphries' analysis can be criticised on at least two counts. First, she has treated all workers as a monolithic group. Hence, workers are only analysed in terms of a single working class, this approach ignores the power of individuals and groups within the society. This is a criticism that can commonly be made of Marxist models.[16] Second, her argument that under capitalism working class women may for the first time be forced out into the labour market (unless a concerted class action prevents this universal proletarianisation) is seemingly not supported by the historical evidence, as authors Scott and Tilly argue.[17]

According to Scott and Tilly working class women have always laboured to improve the family's standard of living, and this work usually took place in the labour market. In fact, they claim that in pre-industrial Europe working class women felt it was their responsibility to bring home wages and peasant males were not prepared to marry women who could not do so.[18] Scott and Tilly argue that as the industrial period developed, the standard of living of workers *temporarily* increased. This enabled parents to send their children to school for longer periods and for some working class wives to adopt the middle class habit of not working in the labour market. However, not all working class families could afford the luxury of a housewife. As the capitalist period developed the temporary gains in living standard brought about by industrialisation were eroded, enabling even fewer working class wives to stay at home.

The development of the capitalist period will eventually lead to an increase in unsatisfying (alienating) and inferior work tasks in the secondary labour markets. Women will be forced back into the labour market to maintain their family's income. They will be slotted into the inferior occupations by the capitalists who recognise that placing women into these tasks, rather than men, dampens the potential political impact of this labour movement (proletarianisation).[20]

The prediction of this neo-Marxist model is that females

are encountering an ever increasing pool of inferior work tasks. This prediction was considered, indirectly, in Chapter 2, 'Participation', where it was found that a dramatically increasing number of women are entering the work force and that these females were finding employment in those occupations and industries traditionally dominated by female employees. In Chapters 3, 4 and 5 it was shown that the female-dominated industries and occupations had on average lower wages, poorer working conditions, less promotion (at least for females) and higher tenure and absenteeism rates. It was also found that these occupations and industries typically had the highest growth rates throughout the economy. These results appear to support the neo-Marxist model.

Feminist power theories

Again, as with neo-Marxism, there are many authors and many models who could be classified as feminist power theorists. One example of a radical feminist power theory is provided by Rubery,[21] who also provides an interesting criticism of other labour market theories.[22]

Rubery bases her own model on the commonly accepted neo-Marxist framework[23] but she deviates from it in order to explicitly consider the role of working class unions in determining the labour market structure. She argues that employees face a continuous threat of displacement of their labour and redundancy of their skills. The workers' only defence is to organise to limit the entry of new labour and the arbitrary actions of management. Internal labour markets with their limited ports of entry, well-defined promotion paths and security against lay offs, provide security for workers and are thus commonly battled for by workers' unions. One of the unions' most effective means of limiting entry is to differentiate the requirements for employment in their work task from those generally required. A classic example of their ability to achieve this bargaining tactic is the concept of skill. Turner claims that workers can be classified as skilled according to whether or not they can deliberately restrict entry into their occupation, regardless of the nature of the occupation itself. Similarly, O'Donnell[24] discusses the skill requirement of a job as merely reflecting the workers' industrial clout, rather than any objective measure of job difficulty or worker productivity. Strong trade unions can succeed in excluding entrants into their nominal training courses and apprenticeship schemes.

Therefore, the problem of control for capitalists is not just one of preventing the development of class consciousness, as the segmentationists claim, but also of organising the social relations of production so that powerful workers will accept the introduction of new technology. Employers will concede internal market structures, despite the inflexibility they create for management, if workers agree to incorporate new technologies. There is a balance between the rigidities of the market structure and the acceptance of technology according to the power bases of the respective parties. Thus, the resulting labour market structure is explicitly an outcome of power bargaining between workers and capitalists.

Women are forced into lowly paid, unsatisfying and generally inferior work tasks because they lack industrial strength. This prevents them from forcing their way into male preferred occupations or creating more secure working arrangements in the occupations they work in. According to Rubery, women lack this industrial clout because, since large scale female employment has only occurred in the last 40 or so years, women have not had time to organise into unions. The large pool of unemployed women seeking work in the female occupations further limits the ability of females to form effective trade unions.

Rubery argues that male unions have discriminated against women because they see them as competition, not because men consider women as inferior human beings, although the tactics these unions use to limit entry, such as the 'skill' criterion, may give this false impression.

Unlike Rubery, Humphries argues that there have always been women working in the labour market. Rubery claims that these women were relatively small in number and could not compete with the strength of the male unions who discriminated against their presence because of the lower wages employers could pay them. Hence, male workers feared that competition from female workers within their occupations would enable employers to force down the male wage to that of the female level. With a small number of available female workers it was easier for male unions to use their normal tactics to exclude females. Only when women began to enter the labour market in large numbers did it become necessary for male unions to campaign for equal wages.

According to Rubery's power based model, women will be more effectively excluded from occupations which have relatively higher rates of male trade unionism. It was found in Chapter 7 that the male-dominated occupations and industries do have the highest rates of male trade unionism. These results appear to support Rubery's model but these figures for trade unionism were not consistent with female employment patterns. Rather an unpredicted pattern formed between female trade union membership and employment in the well represented and female-dominated occupations and industries. Furthermore, women were shown to have greatly increased their trade union membership between 1910 and 1986 and yet there was a negligible change in the occupational segregation of women between 1911 and 1985. This latter finding strongly suggests that Rubery's neo-Marxist feminist power theory is not adequately explaining the dynamics of the Australian labour market.

11

Legislation and affirmative action

The conclusions of Chapters 2 to 7 indicated that women are concentrated into occupations and industries where they receive substantially less in wages. Chapter 4 reveals that a significant disparity in the average wage of men and women (13.07 per cent) is due to employers treating men and women 'differently'. This wage disparity was not due to gender based differences in education, experience, trade union membership, nationality of birth, marital status, region of location, and industry or occupation.

Despite women showing dramatic increases (relative to men) in education levels, length of tenure, participation rates and trade union membership, 82 per cent of Australia's women are still employed in the same few occupations that 84 per cent of their great-grandmothers worked in during 1911. These female-dominated occupations offer lower wage rates, have less promotion (at least for women), are associated with higher turnover rates and greater absenteeism, and are characterised by menial tasks. Women do not appear to be concentrated into these occupations solely by choice; rather, as Riach and Rich's study below found, women do apply to non-traditional female occupations often to meet with employer discrimination.

This strongly suggests that if a society wants to improve the labour market position of women, it cannot rely on the market process alone but must instead take more direct action. In fact, the results of Chapter 3 indicate there will be a less than 1 per cent fall in the segregation of women by the year 2001 if the market process is not interfered with. Anti-discrimination legislation is one possible form of direct action.

Legislation

The *Sex Discrimination Act 1984* was passed by the Federal Parliament in March 1984. It was the third Act in a succession of Federal anti-discrimination legislation. The first Act was the *Racial Discrimination Act 1981* and the second, the *Human Rights Commission Act 1981*.[1] All three Acts are administered by the Human Rights Commission, with complaints concerning sexual discrimination being handled by the Sex Discrimination Commissioner.[2]

The *Sex Discrimination Act 1984* is designed to:

1 promote equality between the sexes
2 eliminate discrimination in specific areas like employment
3 eliminate sexual harassment in the work place and in educational institutions
4 fulfil obligations under the United Nations Convention on the Elimination of All Forms of Discrimination Against Women.[3]

The Act considers that discrimination also includes being treated less favourably because the applicant may have characteristics generally considered to be, or imagined to be, associated with one particular sex, marital status, or pregnancy.

The areas of activity where the anti-discrimination legislation will be especially useful are:

1 employment
2 education
3 providing goods, services and facilities
4 providing accommodation or disposing of land
5 the activities of certain clubs
6 the administration of a Commonwealth law or Commonwealth programmes.

Specifically concerning employment, the Sex Discrimination Act provides that no person can discriminate against another person on the grounds of sex, marital status or pregnancy in employment, including:

1 the offer of a job
2 the terms and conditions of employment

3   the opportunities for promotions, transfer or training
4   dismissing an employee.

Thus, it would appear that this anti-discrimination law is constructed in such a way as to directly consider occupational (or industrial) segregation, as well as the lack of promotional opportunity for women. Nevertheless, effectiveness of the legislation may be limited by the following:

1   The legislation is complaint-based which means that the individual applicant must lodge a complaint against the offender. Complaint-based systems may not be able to cope with the widespread discrimination that was implied by the results of this study. Instead, the legislation may only bring forward a minority of the most overt cases. This is supported by the small numbers of complaints registered, prior to the last Act, and received by the Human Rights Commission in the 1982–83 time period.[4]

2   A woman must prove that she has been in a 'comparable position' to a male applicant before she can claim discrimination under the Act. This implies that the female should have similar education, experience and capabilities to the male applicant. This information is hard to gather and difficult to prove. A recent study by Riach and Rich[5] devised a test method to consider possible discrimination by employers against female (or male) job applicants. Riach and Rich posted carefully matched letters to job advertisements. The letters of application were designed so that the only difference between the application letters was the gender of the applicant. The study found significant discrimination against the female applicants (up to 40 per cent in some job categories). No applicant (man or woman) was notified that their application had failed because of their sex. 'In cases of discrimination it was usual for the candidate declined an interview to receive a standard letter of rejection simply informing that the application had been unsuccessful, with no explanation offered.'[6] Without any proof of discrimination unsuccessful applicants would not be able to lodge complaints under the Anti-Discrimination Act.

3   In a society with severe occupational and industrial seg-

regation women may not have acquired the experience in the traditional male occupations and industries that they may need to apply for jobs. This can also raise difficulties when applicants have to prove 'comparable worth', further hampering the aims of the legislation.[7]

4   The enactment of a law does not necessarily mean that the discriminatory practices will stop. If it is in the interest of employers to hold the wages and conditions of a certain group down, employers may evade the law and deliberately discriminate against that group[8] despite the legislation. The legislation may need publicity and information campaigns to ensure its acceptance and effectiveness.

While the anti-discrimination legislation has made some impression since its enactment,[9] it is nevertheless of limited effectiveness in remedying systemic discrimination. This brings us to a discussion of affirmative action policies since it is often argued that a combination of affirmative action policies and anti-discrimination legislation could be more effective at removing this entrenched discrimination.[10]

Affirmative action

The Department of Prime Minister and Cabinet published a two-volume policy discussion paper concerning affirmative action for women in May 1984.[11] This paper defines affirmative action as an umbrella term for a wide range of programs undertaken by organisations to achieve equal opportunities for women where affirmative action is based on recognition of the belief that it is not sufficient to make specific acts of discrimination unlawful (Thus, relying on anti-discrimination legislation alone will not adequately remove the effects of discrimination.) Further steps are needed to relieve the effects of past discrimination, to eliminate present discrimination and to ensure that future discrimination does not occur.[12]

In February 1986, the *Affirmative Action (Equal Employment Opportunity for Women) Act 1986*[13] was passed through the Australian Federal Parliament. The scope of the Act is being increased from originally applying to employers of more than 1000 employees by 1 February 1987, to employers of more than 500 employees by 1 February 1988, and eventually applying to all employers of more than 100 employees by 1 February 1989.[14] The Act also applies to all institutions of higher education as of 1 October 1986.[15]

Most of the content of the Affirmative Action Act is found in Section 8, sub-section 1, which reads as follows:

8.   *(1) Without limiting the generality of the definition of 'affirmative action program' in sub-section 3 (1), the affirmative action program of a relevant employer shall provide for action to be taken—*

(a)   for the issue to the employees, by a senior officer concerned with the management of the relevant employer, of a statement to the effect that the employer, in accordance with this Act, commenced the development and implementation of an affirmative action program on a specified day, being the operative day in relation to the employer;

(b)   to confer responsibility for the development and implementation of the program (including a continuous review of the program), on a person or persons having sufficient authority and status within the management of the relevant employer to enable the person or persons properly to develop and implement the program;

(c)   to consult with each trade union having members affected by the proposal for the development and implementation of the program . . .;

(d)   to consult with employees of the relevant employer, particularly employees who are women;

(e)   for the collection and recording of statistics and related information concerning employment by the relevant employer, including the number of employees of either sex and the types of jobs undertaken by, or job classifications of, employees of either sex;

(f)   to consider policies, and examine practices, of the relevant employer, in relation to employment matters to identify—

(i)   any policies or practices that constitute discrimination against women; and

(ii)   any patterns (whether ascertained statistically or otherwise) of lack of equality of opportunity in respect of women;

(g) to set objectives[16] and make forward estimates[17] in the program; and

(h) to monitor and evaluate the implementation of the program and to assess the achievement of those objectives and forward estimates.

The Act encourages employers to set goals, based on a recommended statistical breakdown of the workforce.[18] Reports will be presented annually by the employers discussing how successful they have been in reaching their goals. Failure to make such a report can result in the employer being named in Parliament. The Federal Government claims that its use of 'goals' rather than 'quotas' will ensure employers do not feel obligated to promote women above better qualified men.[19] The Prime Minister publicly supports the Act: 'The Government is determined that women should be able to enter and compete in the labour market on an equal footing with men and that outdated prejudices or conventions should not prevent them from fully participating'.[20] The emphasis is clearly on a comparison of merit when deciding between job applicants (and promotion opportunities) rather than considering the applicants' gender.

The Affirmative Action Policy Paper justified affirmative action on three main grounds: equity and justice; the inferior labour force position of women; and economic efficiency.

Affirmative action is designed to act prior to discrimination occurring. In contrast, complaint-based legislation can only deal with discrimination that has already occurred. It should be noted that the Government argues that women will not be given preference over men, rather, the policy paper claims that the program will ensure individuals are treated according to their own merit.

Affirmative action policies aim at pushing forward the positive aspects of a group being discriminated against. The Affirmative Action (Equal Employment for Women) Act 1986 does not stipulate that employers must reach a certain quota of women employment, nor does it specify that preference must be given to women if applicants are otherwise equal. The Australian Act attempts to ensure that employers will collect and review information concerning their respective workforces and the position of women in these work-forces. Furthermore, employers are required to examine practices and policies which may be discriminating against women, and to set goals for the future involvement of their female employees. The Australian Affirmative Action Act is not a 'heavy handed' document: it does not suggest that employers should give preference to women,[21] especially not to women who are not as well qualified as men. Instead, the Act aims to reduce the ignorance that employers may have of the merit of female employees.

If society wants to speed up the anti-discrimination process, there may be a need for affirmative action. Similarly, if society cannot accurately measure the real skills of workers, thereby unjustifiably excluding women from male domin-ated work tasks, affirmative action may be required.

Affirmative action can be criticised on three main grounds: first, on a philosophical level, affirmative action involves government in acting in favour of one group at the expense of another. These practices are often criticised as a visiting of the parents' sins upon the children or, in other words, as reverse discrimination.[22]

The second major criticism of an affirmative action pro-gram is that it is unnecessary. On an empirical level, it may be that discrimination is lessening naturally and there is thus no reason for government intervention. The results of our study suggest that segmentation has shown little change in the last 80 years, implying that market forces alone will not remove segregation (see Chapter 3). This indicates a need for affirmative action.

Third, the success of government intervention may be dubious. 'They [affirmative action programs] thus consti-tute yet another example of costly but ineffective govern-ment regulation...'.[23] As there has not been a consistent affirmative action policy previously applied in Australia, a test of the latter criticism is not available. It would appear that affirmative action programs implemented in the USA have had some success (although, by emphasising quotas, the American affirmative action programs are substantially different to the Australian Act). 'As a result of affirmative action, job opportunities for women and minorities have increased; both women and minorities now have greater employment in higher paying and higher status jobs where they have been traditionally under represented'.[24] Early Australian reports suggest that our affirmative action program will also be effective.[25]

It would seem that action of the type described by the policy paper will have some effect on removing discrimination if the discrimination is a consequence of misinformation and/or role stereotyping.[26] The results of the study suggest that both are occurring,[27] and thus that the proposed affirmative action program is relevant to women in the Australian labour market.

12

Conclusion

This book introduces the reader to a range of economic discussion, both of the position of women in the Australian labour market and of the theories commonly used to explain this position. Chapters 2–7 revealed that women are concentrated within a minority of traditional occupations where they receive lower wages and less promotion. These occupations typically have low levels of trade union membership, high absenteeism and shorter tenure periods. This segregation of women was not linked with the educational levels of women nor could the lower average wage of women be accounted for by women having different work experience and behaviour than men.

The book considered twelve of the major labour market theories: the human capital, taste, search, screening, intrafirm segmentation, market efficiency, monopsonistic competition, overcrowding, regional segmentation, segmented labour market, neo-Marxist and feminist power theories. Of these theories only two did not contradict the data presented in Chapters 2–7: the neo-Marxist and the monopsonistic competition[1] theories. Both theories assume that the employer has a large degree of market power which they can use to discriminate against women. This is a clear example of a lack of competition between employers in the labour market and can be solved in at least two ways. First, a direct solution to employers discriminating against female employees is to remove the source of those employers' market power.[2] This is a difficult remedy to enact as it challenges strong political bases and involves structural change throughout the economy. The second solution is to enact legislation outlawing the employers' use of their market power to discriminate against women. Australia has already introduced such legislation, with the Sex Discrimination Act 1984 and the Affirmative Action (Equal Employment for Women) 1986 Act. The combined use of these Acts should decrease the level of discrimination in the labour market.

While the *ability* to discriminate stems from market power, the explanation for *why* women are discriminated against is a much more difficult question. Understanding the market position of women can help us to clarify that women are discriminated against and the extent of this discrimination, but it does not help us to understand why women are treated differently to men. This is a far deeper social problem than any discussed here.

Notes

1 Introduction

1 Donald E. Lewis 'The Measurement of the Occupational and Industrial Segregation of Women' *Journal of Industrial Relations* 24, September 1982, pp. 406–432. This quote continues: 'Until this is done and a consensus begins to emerge it will be difficult for governments to initiate programs to substantially lessen segregation. Unfortunately, a continuation of past trends will mean that even by the year 2001 segregation by sex will be nearly as widespread and as systematic as it is today' (p. 418).

2 Participation

1 Sandra Eccles 'The Role of Women in The Australian Labour Market: A Survey of the Literature' *Journal of Industrial Relations* 24, September 1982, pp. 315–36. This article provides an excellent survey of the Australian research in this field.

2 Table 2.1 and Figure 2.1 are updated versions of those provided by Eccles, 1982 *ibid*, p. 317. The updated estimates come from the ABS *The Labour Force, Australia, No 6203* Table 1, May 1984, p. 10 and Table 1, May 1987, p. 18–19.

3 Michael Anderson and Brent Ross 'Labour Force Projections and Tables of Working Life: A Preliminary Investigation' *Paper presented to the 16th Conference of Economists* Surfers Paradise, Australia, August 1987.

4 Whereas male participation rates will fall to become 71.9% in 2001. See Anderson and Ross, 1987 *ibid*.

5 Based on data presented by Eccles, 1982, p. 317.

6 Figure 2.2 is an updated version of a similar diagram presented by Eccles. The 1966 and 1976 census data is cited by Eccles, 1982 p. 318. The 1987 estimated data comes from the ABS *The Labour Force, Australia, No 6203* May 1987.

7 In 1966 the participation rate for married women 20–24 years old was 36.7%, while for the 25–30 year age group it was only 25.7%. In 1987 married women aged 20–24 years had a participation rate of 59.4%, while the rate for 25–30 years was 54%.

8 The data used in Figure 2.3 comes from ABS *Labour Statistics Australia, 1985, No 6101* 1986 and ABS, *The Labour Force, No. 6203* May 1987, p. 18. The data used for the years prior to 1986 included an estimate of the female population that was married, for 1972–82 this proportion was taken as 59.2%, from 1983–85 it was set at 57.2%. The data for 1986 and 1987 included actual numbers of married women so that estimating was not necessary.

9 From 79.6% in 1972, to 75.8% in 1977, 71.9% in 1982, and again falling to 70.1% in 1987.

10 Rising from 2.8% in 1972 to become 4.0% in 1977, 4.8% in 1982, and further rising to 5.3% in 1987, an overall increase of 1.9%.

11 From 14.5% in 1972 to 18.8% in 1977, to 19.1% in 1982, and to 23.1% in 1987, an overall increase of 8.6%.

12 These rates rose from 11.0% in 1972 to 14.8% in 1977, to 15.6% in 1982, and 18.7% in 1987, an overall increase of 7.7%.

13 Peter Dawkins and Keith Norris 'Casual Employment in Australia' *Paper presented to the 16th Conference of Economists* Brisbane, Australia, August 1987.

14 *ibid.*, p. 22.

15 This issue is discussed in Chapter 7, 'Unemployment'. For discussion of discouraged workers see W. J. Merrilees 'Married Women In The Labour Force: A Note On Discouraged Workers' *Australian Economic Papers* December 1979, pp. 365–7. Married women were not eligible for CES unemployment benefits, thus they did not have the same incentive as males to actively seek work. This had a dual effect as the majority of married women did not appear in the CES statistics. See John Steinke 'Measurement of Unemployment in Australia' *Journal of Industrial Relations* 20, 2, 1978. pp. 140–62. Janet L. Johnson 'Sex Differentials In Unemployment: A Case For No Concern' *Journal of Political Economy* 91, 2, 1983, pp. 293–303.

16 Data for Tables 2.2 and 2.3 comes from ABS *Labour Statistics Australia, 1985, No 6101* 1986.

17 Figure 2.4 is an updated version of that presented by Donald E. Lewis, 'The Measurement and Interpretation of the Segregation of Women in the Workplace', *Journal of Industrial Relations*, 25, 1983, pp. 347–352. Updated with data from the ABS *Labour Statistics Australia, 1985, No 6101* 1986 and ABS *The Labour Force Australia, No 6203* May 1987.

18 Daniel C. Quinlan and Jean A. Shackelford 'Labour Force Participation Rates of Women and the Rise of the Two Earner Family' *American Economic Review* 70, 2, May 1980, pp. 209–13. This article discusses the difficulties involved in using regression analysis to test the hypothesis that the increase in female employment is due to increased demand in traditionally female occupations.

19 For further discussion and possible explanations of this increase in the female labour force see Donald E. Lewis and Brett Shorten, 'Female Participation in the Australian Labour Force' *Australian Bulletin of Labour* 13, 4, 1987, pp. 237–63.

3 Segregation

1 *The Macquarie Dictionary* rev. edn, Macquarie Library Pty Ltd, NSW Australia, (1985).

2 Donald E. Lewis 'The Measurement of the Occupational and Industrial Segregation of Women' *Journal of Industrial Relations* 24, September 1982, pp. 406–23.

3 As cited and discussed by Margaret Power 'Women's Work Is Never Done By Men: A Socio-Economic Model Of Sex Typing In Occupations' *Journal of Industrial Relations* 17, 2, September 1975(b), pp. 225–39. Further discussion is provided in Margaret Power 'The Making Of A Woman's Occupation' *Hecate* 1, July 1975(a), pp. 25–34. It should be noted that this table was updated with monthly survey data, rather than Census data as was used by Power. This may have the effect of under representing non-urban occupational distributions and will provide less accurate figures overall. However, it is believed that it will not substantially alter the analysis.

4 Table 3.1 is an updated version of that provided by Power, 1975b *ibid*. Power's table (p. 227) provides the data for 1911 to 1971. The data for 1975, 1980 and 1985 was taken from the ABS *Labour Statistics Australia, 1985, No 6101*, Table 3.8, 1986, p. 45.

5 Margaret Power uses Census data which avoids some of the difficulties encountered with ABS surveying techniques. For further discussion of the discouraged worker effect amongst married women see Merrilees, 1979, *op. cit.*

6 For discussion of the increases in the participation rates of females in the labour force see Daniel C. Quinlan and Jean A. Shackelford 'Labour Force Participation Rates of Women and the Rise of the Two Earner Family' *American Economic Review* 70, 2, May 1980, pp. 209–13 and June O'Neill 'A Time Series of Women's Labor Force Participation' *American Economic Review* 71, 2, May 1981 pp. 76–80.

7 It should be noted that females have not only increased their participation rates, but a substantial proportion of these women have been employed. Discussed further in Chapter 7. For references on participation rates see previous end note. Considering unemployment see Janet L. Johnson 'Sex Differentials In Unemployment: A Case For No Concern' *Journal of Political Economy* 91, 2, 1983, pp. 293–303. B. D. Haig and M. P. Wood 'A Simulation Study of Married Women In The Australian Work Force 1961–72' *Australian Economic Papers* December 1976, pp. 171–85. Beth Niemi, 'The Female-Male Differential In Employment Rates' *Industrial and Labour Relations Review* 27, 3, April 1974, pp. 331–50. Niemi concludes that females suffer less unemployment during recessions because they are concentrated in the service industries.

8 T. Karmel and M. Maclachlan 'Sex Segregation—Increasing or Decreasing?' *Paper presented to the 16th Conference of Economists*, Brisbane, Australia, August 1987. Karmel and Maclachlan devise a new index which, they argue, removes many of the difficulties

found with many of the indexes which we will discuss at the end of this Chapter.

9   Note that the data in Table 3.1 also shows an increase in segregation between 1966 and 1985. However, in the 74 year time span being studied this increase does not represent an obvious trend pattern.

10   Data taken from ABS *The Labour Force Australia, No 6203*, Table 29, May 1984, p. 27.

11   See ABS catalogue for definition of 'negligible'. *ibid.* p. 27.

12   66.2% of these women are married

13   Of which 75.6% are married women

14   Addison and Siebert, 1979 *op. cit.*, discuss a simpler index (p. 212–14). Their index differs from the index presented because it lacks any weighting for differences in labour force participation.

15   $$Rf = \frac{\Sigma_i \, Lm_i}{\Sigma_i \, Lf_i} \times \frac{\Sigma_i \, [(Lf_i/L_i) \, . \, Em_i]}{\Sigma_i \, [(Lm_i/L_k) \, . \, Em_i]}$$

Where: Lm_i is the number of men in the ith occupation.
            Lf_i is the number of women in the ith occupation.
            L_i is the number of people in the ith occupation.
            $\Sigma \, Lm_i$ is the number of men in all occupations.
            $\Sigma_i \, Lf_i$ is the number of women in all occupations.
            Em_i is the mean male weekly earnings (adult, full time) for occupation i.

$\Sigma_i \, (Lf_i/L_i) \, . \, Em_i$ is the total earnings that women would receive if they are paid the male wage for each occupation. Similarly, Σ_i $(Lm_i/L_i) \, . \, Em_i$ is the total earnings received by men. The ratio of the two will reflect differences in labour force participation rates between men and women as well as any dispersion in total earnings due to women being segmented into lower paying occupations. To balance out the effect of differences in labour force participation, the index was weighted with the ratio of male to female participation rates $(\Sigma_i \, Lm_i/\Sigma_i \, Lf_i)$. This allows for women being some third of the total labour force.

16   The crude occupational blockings used were taken from ABS No. 6310, 1983, *op. cit.* pp. 8–9

17   See total values for each occupation in ABS No. 6203 *op. cit.* May 1984, p. 27.

18   R. G. Gregory and R. C. Duncan 'Segmented Labour Market Theories and the Australian Experience of Equal Pay for Women' *Journal of Post Keynesian Economics* 3, 3, Spring 1981, pp. 403–29. Peter Linneman 'The Economic Impacts of Minimum Wage Laws: A New Look At An Old Question' *Journal of Political Economy* 90, 3, 1982, pp. 443–69. Linneman argues that the greatest beneficiaries of increasing the minimum wage for females were male union members, the greatest losers are females since they face higher unemployment. And R. H. Meyer and D. A. Wise 'Discontinuous Distributions' *Econometrica* 51, 6, November 1983, pp. 1677–98. P. A. McGavin 'Equal Pay for Women: A

Reassessment of the Australian Experience' *Australian Economic Papers* 22, June 1983, pp. 48–59. Also P. A. McGavin 'Equal Pay for Women: A Postscript' *Australian Economic Papers* 22, June 1983, pp. 65–7. McGavin criticises this conclusion, he argues that the implementation of the equal pay legislation decreased the trend rate of increasing employment for women which was occurring in the seventies. McGavin also claims that the female employment that has occurred has been in inferior part-time jobs and in non-market orientated employment sectors.

19   Addison and Siebert, 1979 *op. cit.* discuss this index on pp. 212–14, especially footnote 31 on p. 214.

20   The Addison and Siebert index is:

$$\frac{L'_{ijk}}{L_{jk}} = \frac{L_{ij}}{L_j} \text{ therefore } L'_{ijk} = \frac{L_{ij}}{L_j} \times L_{jk}$$

Where: L_{ij} is the number of those with j education level in occupation i.

L_j is the total number with that education level.

L_{jk} is the total of the gender group, k, with that education level.

L'_{ijk} is the number of each gender group that would be in that occupation if employment was totally determined by the applicant's educational acquisitions.

21   ABS No 6235 1987

22   With the exception of some trade qualifications, the measures of education used in these calculations are of general education rather than job specific education.

23   The significance of this conclusion is even greater when the reader considers the difficulties encountered by some females who attempt to acquire qualifications in what may be considered typically male spheres. See Affirmative Action Resource Unit 'Strategies for Employers for Supporting Female Apprentices in Non-Traditional Trades' *Affirmative Action Issues* Paper No 1, Department of Prime Minister and Cabinet, Canberra, January 1985.

24   In Table 3.3 the values for 1971–72 and 1977–78 come from: Hazel Moir and Joy Selby-Smith 'Industrial Segregation in the Australian Labour Market' *Journal of Industrial Relations* 21, September 1979, pp. 281–91. The values for 1984 and 1987 have been added from ABS No 6203 May 1984, Table 24, p. 24, and ABS No. 6203 May 1987, Table 27, p. 37.

25   Moir and Selby Smith, 1979.

26   60.2% of females were employed in female-dominated industries in 1987 compared to 31.1% of males being employed in male-dominated industries in the same year.

27   In 1984 female industries made up some 27.8% of total industry, however they employ some 38.4% of the total work force. On the other hand, male-dominated industries made up some 36% of total industries and employ only 22.4% of the total workforce.

28 Donald E. Lewis 'The Measurement of the Occupational and Industrial Segregation of Women' *Journal of Industrial Relations* 24, September 1982, pp. 406–23. Index on p. 410. The findings of this index are updated in Donald E. Lewis 'The Measurement and Interpretation of the Segregation of Women in the Workforce' *Journal of Industrial Relations* 25, September 1983, pp. 347–52.

$$S_{ij} = \frac{1}{2} \sum_{i=1}^{n} \sum_{j=1}^{m} \left| M_i - F_i \right|$$

Where   n is the number of occupations
        m is the number of industries
        m_i is the number of men employed in occupation i (or industry j)
        f_i is the number of women employed in occupation i (or industry j)
        M is the total number of men employed
        F is the total number of women employed
        M_i is the ratio of men in an occupation, m_i, (or industry j) to the total number of men employed, M. Thus, $M_i = m_i/M$, similarly $F_i = f_i/F$.

29 Lewis 1983
30 Lewis cites the Duncan-Duncan index from O.D. Duncan and B. Duncan 'A Methodological Analysis of Segregation Indexes' *American Sociological Review* 20, April 1955, pp. 210–17. The Duncan-Duncan index for industrial and occupational segregation is:

$$\left(S_i = \frac{1}{2} \sum_{i=1}^{n} \left| M_i - F_i \right| \right. \text{ and similarly for j)} \text{ and his own combinated}$$
segregation index.

Since the Duncan-Duncan index is designed to only be interested in composition effects, it is necessary to try to filter out potential mix effects.

To distinguish between the effects of disaggregation and time Lewis estimated the following log-linear equation;

$$S_i = a_0 \, n^{a1} \, t^{a2}$$

Where: S_i is the Duncan-Duncan index of occupational segregation
         n is the number of occupational categories
         t is the year of observation

Similarly, for industries:

$$S_j = a_0 \, m^{a1} \, t^{a2}$$

Where: S_j is the Duncan-Duncan index of industrial segregation
         m is the number of industrial categories
         t is the year of observation

The coefficients (a_0, a_1, a_2, ...) can be interpreted as elasticities, where elasticities are measures of the extent of relative movements between two events. For occupational segregation, increasing the number of occupations (n) will lead to an increase in occupational segregation (n^{a1}). Lewis found the values of the coefficients with respect to occupational segregation, to be 3.633 for a_0, 0.162 for a_1 and -0.04 for a_2. Thus, a ten per cent increase in the number of occupational categories will lead to a 1.62 per cent increase in the index of segregation. A ten per cent increase in time period being studied will lead to a 0.40 per cent decrease in occupational segregation.

For industrial segregation he found a_0 to be 5.845, a_1 to be 0.168 and a_2 to be -0.635. Therefore, the effect on industrial segregation of changing the number of categories has a similar influence on the index as was found for occupational segregation. Interestingly, the larger value for a_2 signifies that industrial segregation is falling at a much faster rate than is occupational segregation. An increase in the time span by 10 per cent will lead to a fall in industrial segregation of 6.35 per cent which is considerably larger than the 0.4 per cent decrease found for occupational segregation.

Once the coefficients are estimated the signs of the first and second partial derivatives of the log linear equations can be determined. These values are calculated because they can supply the analyst with the direction (either increased or decreased) of changes. Hence:

$$\frac{dS_i}{dn} > 0 \ ; \ \frac{dS_i}{dt} < 0 \ ;$$

$$\frac{d^2S_i}{dn^2} < 0 \ ; \ \frac{d^2S_i}{dt^2} > 0 \ ;$$

Where i can be replaced with j to denote industries.

These partial derivatives indicate that as the number of occupation categories increases the value of the index increases ($dS_i/dn > 0$). However, the size of these increments in the index will be diminishing ($d^2S_i/d^2n < 0$). The partial derivatives with respect to time signify a drop in segregation as time increases ($dS_i/dt < 0$) but that segregation is falling at a decreasing rate ($d^2S_i/d^2t > 0$).

31 There is a further difficulty with changes in the definitions of occupations here, not only have occupations been split up into smaller groupings but they have also been reallocated by the changes in definitions. An earlier occupational category may include quite different employee groups. This creates a difficulty in distinguishing between 'composition and mix' effects which the reader should be aware of. The influence of a change in sexual proportions by occupation or by industry groups is called the composition effect. The influence of change in the structure or distribution of occupations or industries is called the mix effect. For further discussion see Bureau of Labour Market Research 'Structural Change and the Labour Market' *BLMR Research Re-*

port No 11. AGPS, Canberra, 1987. Discussion of indexes which can distinguish between the two effects is provided in Karmel and Maclachan (1987) and Prithwis Das Gupta 'Comment on Suzanne M. Bianchi and Nancy Rytina's "The Decline in Occupational Sex Segregation in the 1970s: Census and CPS Comparisons" *Demography* 24, 2, May 1987, pp. 291–5.

32 For criticism see P. A. McGavin, 'The Measurement of Occupational and Industrial Segregation of Women: A Re-appraisal' *Journal of Industrial Relations* 24, 1983, pp. 339–45. McGavin argues that Lewis's use of the term 'segregation' should be replaced with 'concentration' and argues that Lewis's log-linear estimators do not supply predictions but rather merely projections of past trends which are irrelevant due to the great changes which are taking place in the labour market. McGavin further criticises Lewis's measurements for being incapable of distinguishing between composition and mix effects. He concludes that Lewis's measures cannot be used to indicate the incidence of sexual discrimination in employment, rather, the analyst needs to evaluate job and workforce characteristics and changes therein.

4   Wages and earnings

1 Such as the Human Capital model which is discussed in Chapter 8.

2 R. G. Gregory and R. C. Duncan 'Segmented Labour Market Theories and the Australian Experience of Equal Pay for Women *Journal of Post Keynesian Economics* 3, 3, Spring 1986, pp. 403–29. Gregory and Duncan present this table up to and including 1977. They quote ABS *Wage Rate Indexes, No. 6314*, and *Earnings and Hours of Employees, No. 6304*, various issues, as sources. The table has been updated from 1976, our figures differ due to the presence of public service employees in the data (brackets are placed around these figures to remind the reader of this). The sources were: ABS *Earnings and Hours of Employees, No. 6304* Table 11, August 1983, p. 12. ABS '*Award Rates of Pay Indexes*', *No. 6312* Table 6, June 1984, p. 12, ABS *Labour Statistics, No. 6101*, Table 6.11, 1983, p. 71. The index used for the minimum award wage is based on the average quarterly wage for 1976.

3 *ibid.* See Gregory and Duncan, for discussion of Table 4.1 and for the historical description of award wage determinations.

4 *ibid.* p. 411

5 To quote the Commonwealth Concilliation and Arbitration Commission (1972),

> ... *work value comparisons should, where possible, be made between female and male classifications within the award under consideration. But where such comparisons are unavailable or inconclusive, as may be the case where the work is performed exclusively by females, it may be necessary to take into account comparisons of work value between female classifications within an award and/or comparisons of work value between female*

classifications in different awards. In some cases comparisons with male classifications in other awards may be necessary...

As cited in Clare Burton, with Raven Hag and Gay Thompson *Pay Equity and Evaluation in Australia* Canberra: AGPS, 1987, p. 1. However, it would seem that the Commission did not go so far as to implement the 'comparative worth' criteria implied in the last line of the above quote: 'This suggestion contained in this last sentence was never followed and it would appear likely that some highly intensive female occupations...never received equal pay', Christine Short 'Equal Pay—What Happened?' *Journal of Industrial Relations* 28, 3, September 1986, pp. 315–35. Quote from p. 319.

6   For discussion see Elaine Sorensen 'Effect of Comparative Worth Policies on Earnings' *Industrial Relations* 26, 3, Fall 1987, pp. 227–39.

7   Cited in 'Women's Earnings' *Women at Work* Women's Bureau, Department of Employment and Industrial Relations, April 1987, pp. 4–5.

8   *ibid*. p. 5

9   Authors such as Walter Oi argue that the introduction of a comparable worth criterion would only be applicable to large scale employers. Moreover, he argues that the introduction of the comparable worth criterion would actually harm the majority of female workers. Oi bases his argument on a belief that increasing the wage in female occupations will decrease employment opportunities for women. Discussion of Table 4.2 in this Chapter suggests that this fall in employment will not occur. See Walter Oi 'Neglected Women and Other Implications of Comparable Worth' *Contemporary Policy Issues* 4, 2, 1986, pp. 20–32. Especially pp. 22–7.

10   *Australian Bulletin of Labour*, 12, 2, p. 90

11   The data for private sector employees was not available.

12   Or that, in some instances women are working in areas where awards are not adequately policed.

13   Another explanation may be that the awards of many occupations place explicit exemptions on the work that women can carry out, creating a situation where males can be more flexible, and potentially more productive, employees. See The Women's Bureau, Department of Education and Training *1986 Survey of Sex-Differentiating Provisions in Federal Awards* Canberra, 1987.

14   Data for Table 4.2 came from Gregory and Duncan, 1981, and the ABS, No 6101 1983, *op. cit.* Tables 6.11 and 6.13.

15   Bruce J. Chapman, 'Sex Differences in Earnings: Changes over the 1970s in the Australian Public Service', prepared for presentation in B. J. Chapman, J. E. Isaac and J. R. Niland (eds) *Australian Labour Economics Readings*, third edn, MacMillan Company of Australia Pty Ltd, Sydney 1984 (a). Bruce J. Chapman, 'Sex and Location Differences in Wages in the Australian Public Service' *Australian National University, Discussion Paper No 98* Centre for Economic Policy Research, July 1984(b).

16 Chapman, 1984(b), explicitly considers regional and sexual differences in salary levels. He concludes that Canberra employees (of both sexes) receive higher salaries than do their counterparts employed in the state branches. Futhermore, he finds that this salary differential cannot be fully explained by educational differences. While this regional difference in salaries is obviously important, especially if females face limited regional mobility, the study concentrates on sexual differences in salaries.

17 As is discussed in Chapter 8, 'Orthodox Theories: Human Capital'.

18 Chapman, 1984(b), see Appendix one, pp. 31–3 for the source of, and fuller explanations of, these calculations.

The human capital function can be written as:

$$E_t = E_{t-1} + rC_{t-1} \qquad \text{eqn 4.31}$$

Where: E_t is gross earnings in period t

C_{t-1} is the dollar amount of net investment in skills (human capital) in period $t - 1$

r is the average rate of return to the individual's investment in human capital

If the ratio of investment expenditures to gross earnings C_t/E_t is given by k_t, then, by viewing investment in time equivalent units:

$$E_t = E_{t-1} (1 + rk_{t-1}) \qquad \text{eqn 4.2}$$

Since $E_t = E_0 (1 + rk_0) \ldots (1 + rk_{t-1})$

and since $\ln(1 + rk) = rk$ for small values of rk, equation 4.2 can be written as:

$$\ln E_t = n E_0 + r \sum_{i=0}^{t-1} k_i \qquad \text{eqn 4.3}$$

Analysing schooling and post school experience, it is possible to separate the k terms, giving:

$$\ln E_t = nE_0 + r \sum_{i=0}^{s-1} k_i + r \sum_{j=s}^{t-1} k_j \qquad \text{eqn 4.4}$$

If the tuition fees are equal to the student's earnings then $k^i = 1$ throughout.

$$\ln E_t = nE_0 + rs + r \sum_{j=s}^{t-1} k_j \qquad \text{eqn 4.5}$$

Where s is the number of years of schooling.

Given that post school investments are expected to decline over the lifetime (as retirement approaches, the expected return from investment falls) then the last equation may be approximated with the inclusion of quadratic experience terms. Thus the estimating equation becomes:

$$\ln W_i = a + bS_i + cGEXP_i + dGEXP_i^2 + e_0JEX_i + f_0JEX_i^2 + \varepsilon$$

Where, for individual i:

$\ln W_i$ is the natural logarithm of the wage

S_i is the years in schooling

$GEXP_i$ is the length of time in the labour force

JEX_i is the length of time in the clerical administrative division

ε is the error term which is assumed to be randomly distributed with zero mean

b, c, d, e_0, f_0 are coefficients

19 Table 4.3 is a replica of Chapman's table, see Chapman, 1984(b), p. 4.

20 For Table 4.4 see Chapman, 1984(b), p. 16.

21 Chapman's discussion of this estimate is unclear as he writes that the estimate is likely to be biased downward due to its being applied to a group who have had very continuous labour force attachment, yet he does not seem to fully discuss the significance of an employer using such an estimate. Chapman, 1984(b), p. 19.

22 For Table 4.5 see Chapman, 1984(b), p. 20.

23 Chapman, 1984(b), pp.19–20. A difficulty confronting Chapman's analysis is a problem common to all regression estimates based on the Human Capital model. This difficulty lies in determining the direction of the causal relationship between turnover and wage rates. The Human Capital model explicitly assumes that high turnover rates will cause low wage rates. However, as is discussed in the next Chapter, turnover and absenteeism may be determined by poor working conditions as well as low wage rates (which is the reverse causality than that suggested by the human capital model). If low wage rates do cause high turnover rates then the use of a variable measuring general labour market experience to estimate the wage level may be tautological.

24 B. D. Haig 'Sex Discrimination in the Reward for Skills and Experience in the Australian Labour Force' *Economic Record* 58, 160, March 1982, pp. 1–10. See in particular footnote 5 on p. 4 where Haig mentions weighting the female married age. Haig's model requires a measure of work experience for males and females within occupations. Thus, he requires relative turnover rates for males and females by occupation. The available ABS data for turnover by occupation only considers very crude separations which Haig rejects. Instead he uses the worker's age as a proxy for work experience, and thereby job specific skills. However, he immediately weights the age of married females downward on the assumption that they have higher turnover rates than males. This assumption will provide the conclusion that females have lower wages because they have less work experience. If he had made the opposite assumption that females have the same turnover rates as males, he may have found that the lower female wages cannot be explained by differentials in education (as was found for Chapman's 1984b study).

25 Craig A. Olson and Brian E. Becker 'Sex Discrimination in the Promotion Process' *Industrial and Labor Relations Review* 36, 4, July 1983, pp. 624–41. Olson and Becker conclude that women face higher promotion standards than do men with equal mea-

sured abilities. Also, Maryellan R. Kelley 'Discrimination in Seniority Systems: A Case Study' *Industrial And Labor Relations Review* 36, 1, October 1982, pp. 40–5, Kelley concludes that women and blacks are placed into short promotion ladders with highly restricted horizontal movements across ladders, overcrowding etc. The low upper boundaries of these ladders mean women with longer work experiences miss out on promotions which instead go to younger men on superior job ladders.

26   For Tables 4.6 and 4.7 see Department of Prime Minister and Cabinet *Affirmative Action For Women: A Policy Discussion Paper*, 1 and 2, Canberra: AGPS, May 1984.

27   *Australian Public Service Statistical Year Book. 1985–86* Canberra: AGPS, 1986. Data taken from Table 52, pp. 63–64. The divisional categories have been changed since 1983 making comparison difficult, especially with the third and fourth divisions.

28   For further discussion see O'Donnell 1982, pp. 100–30.

29   This result initially appears to support the model of Intra-Firm Segmentation, discussed in Chapter 9, according to which females are channelled into job ladders with very short promotional possibilities.

30   Bruce J. Chapman, and Charles Mulvey 'An Analysis of the Origins of Sex Differences in Australian Wages' *Journal of Industrial Relations* 28, 4, December 1986, pp. 504–20.

31   *ibid.* Chapman and Mulvey (1986) use a complicated estimating procedure, based on reduced form estimates. The data used by Chapman and Mulvey was taken from the ABS *Special Supplementary Survey No. 4 (SSS4)* 1982.

32   *ibid.* p. 513

33   *ibid.* p. 505

34   *ibid.* p. 505

5   Turnover and absenteeism

1   Data for Table 5.1 comes from the ABS *Labour Force Statistics, 1982, No. 6101* Table 3.12, 1983, p. 31, and Table 3, 1986 p. 14. Also from ABS *Labour Mobility, No 6209* Table 17, February 1983, p. 17, and Table 3, February 1986, p. 8. When estimating tenure the mid-point of each period was used (hence for a period of 3–6 months, 4.5 months was used), except for the 5 year and over period which was set at 60 months. It should be noted that the latter has the effect of biasing the length of male tenure downward.

2   Australian studies on male and female tenure rates are rare, see Lewis 1979. A more recent study is provided by Bruce J. Chapman, 'Sex Differences in Labour Turnover in the Australian Public Service' *Centre for Economic Policy Research, ANU Discussion Papers, No. 118* April 1985.

3   Chapman, 1985, pp. 2–3

4   Data for Table 5.2 came from ABS *No 6209*, 1983. Please note, data in Table 5.2 uses the period of 10 years and over, this is set

at 120 months and biases male tenure downward. (Table 5.1 uses 60 months as the longest tenure period, thus the downward bias on male tenure is lessened in Table 5.2.)

5 $$Rf = \frac{\Sigma_{oc} \left[(F_{1f}/P_{1f}) \times P_{oc} \times T_{foc} \right]}{\Sigma_{oc} \left[(M_{1f}/P_{1f}) \times P_{oc} \times T_{moc} \right]} \times \frac{M_{1f}}{F_{1f}}$$

Where: F_{1f} (M_{1f}) is the female (male labour force for the entire economy

P_{1f} is the total labour force for the entire economy

P_{oc} is the total labour force for each occupation

T_{foc} is the average length of female tenure in each occupation

m can be substituted for f to denote the male measure

6 For discussion of the extent of occupational segregation by sex in Australia see Chapter 3, 'Segregation'.

7 Sheldon E. Haber, Enrique J. Larnas and Gordon Green 'A New Method of Estimating Job Separations by Sex and Race' *Monthly Labour Review* June 1983, pp. 20–7. Haber et al. found that in America the separation rate for women is the same or less than that of males when the wage rate is taken into account. The analogy between this article and our own findings is obvious when the link found with the occupational segregation of females into low paying jobs is considered. See also Donald E. Lewis 'Comparative Quit Rates of Men and Women' *Journal of Industrial Relations* 21, September 1979, pp. 331–50.

8 Lewis, 1979.

9 Bergmann, 1980 p. 353

10 Bruce Chapman studied absenteeism among South Australian teachers in an unpublished study at Adelaide University. He concluded that there was insignificant difference once wages etc. were considered. See Bruce J. Chapman and Pat McKeen, 'Absenteeism of South Australian Teachers' *Mimeo, Flinders University of South Australia* 1975. For a more recent study see Peter Kenyon and Peter Dawkins 'Explaining Labour Absence in Australia' *Murdoch University, Economics Programme Working Papers, No 1* August 1987. The Kenyon and Dawkins study did not reach 'compelling' conclusions regarding the absenteeism of women as in most cases the coefficients estimated for female absenteeism were lower than the standard errors involved.

11 The census asks one question, question 35, which deals with absenteeism. However this question is seemingly poorly answered and allows for little comparison. The majority of ABS surveys including absenteeism present similar difficulties. For instance see ABS *Labour Force Experience, No. 6206*, Table 21, February 1983, p. 21, and the *Labour Force No. 6203*, Table 16, May 1984, p. 19.

12 ABS *Health Survey 1977–78, No 4311* 1979. And ABS, *Health Survey, 1983, No 4311* 1986.

13 Data for Table 5.3 comes from ABS No 4311 1986.

14 These high rates of absenteeism in the male-dominated, manual occupations may be explained by the physical risks involved in these occupations and the availability of workers' compensation.

15 Data for Table 5.4 comes from ABS *Australian Health Survey 1977–78: Days of Reduced Activity Due to Illness or Injury, No 4321* 1981, p. 15. Unfortunately, the data from the 1983 Health Survey was not yet available when this book went to press.

16 Lynn Paringer 'Women and Absenteeism: Health or Economics' *American Economic Review* 73, 2, pp. 123–38, May 1983. Paringer found that within an occupation, females have less absenteeism than males and that this tendency increases for women with families and lessens with age. Similarly Ida Russakoff Hoss, 'The Impact of Office Automation on Workers' *International Labour Review* 80, October 1960. Hoss found that automation has led to increased alienation amongst office workers and hence higher rates of absenteeism. J. Paul Leigh, 'Sexual Differences in Absenteeism' *Industrial Relations* 22, 3, Fall 1983, pp. 349–61. Leigh claims that females have higher absenteeism than males. However, he makes the common mistake of including clerical workers as white collar employees. On an overall level his conclusion is dubious. See George Sayers Bain and Robert Price, 'Who is a White Collar Employee?' *British Journal of Industrial Relations* 10, 3, 1972, pp. 325–39. And for an alternative view point see Richard M. Steers and Susan R. Rhodes, 'Major Influences on Employee Attendance: A Process Model' *Journal of Applied Psychology* 63, 4, 1978, pp. 391–401. This article argues that absenteeism is not primarily caused by job dissatisfaction and that absenteeism does not share common roots with turnover. An article arguing along similar lines is Nigel Nicholson, Colin A. Brown and J. K. Chadwick-Jones 'Absence from Work and Job Satisfaction' *Journal of Applied Psychology* 61, 6, 1976, pp. 728–37.

6 Trade unionism

1 A very influential summary of some of these earlier studies is provided in H. G. Lewis *Unionism and Relative Wages in the United States: An empirical Study* Chicago: The University of Chicago Press, 1963.

2 Frances Baldwin and Sue Walpole *Women, Affirmative Action and Industrial Democracy*, Working Environment Branch, Department of Employment and Industrial Relations Canberra: AGPS, 1986.

3 *ibid.* p. 13

4 *ibid.* p. 12

5 Data for Figure 6.1 was taken from D. Plowman (1978) as cited in Eccles, Sandra 'The Role of Women in the Labour Market: A Survey of the Literature' *Journal of Industrial Relations* 24, September 1982, pp. 315–36. And from ABS *Trade Union Statistics, No. 6323* Table 6.1, April 1984 and 1986, p. 3.

6 This increase in female unionism may be linked to increased

unionism amongst clerical workers throughout the seventies. See Russell Lansbury 'The Growth and Unionization of White Collar Workers in Australia: Some Recent Trends' *Journal of Industrial Relations* 19, March 1977, pp. 34–49. Also Gerard Griffin, 'Personal Characteristics and Industrial Militancy in White Collar Unions' *Journal of Industrial Relations* 23, June 1981, pp. 274–81. Griffin considers increased unionism in the banking and insurance industries throughout the seventies. These are industries we found to have increased female participation throughout the seventies.

7 Carol O'Donnell, and Phillippa Hall, (1988) *Getting Equal: Labour Market Regulation and Women's Work* Sydney: Allen & Unwin pp. 38–9.

8 'Women and Earning' *Women at Work*. Women's Bureau, Department of Employment, Education and Training, Office of the Status of Women, Canberra: AGPS, April 1987, p. 12.

9 Data for Table 6.1 from ABS *Trade Union Members, Australia, No 6325* Table 5, August 1986, p. 12.

10 Data for Table 6.2 from ABS No 6325, Table 3, August 1986, p. 10.

11 Donald E. Lewis 'The Measurement of the Occupational and Industrial Segregation of Women' *Journal of Industrial Relations* 24, September 1982, pp. 406–23. An excellent historical summary is provided by Margaret Power in 'Women's Work Is Never Done By Men: A Socio-Economic Model Of Sex Typing In Occupations' *Journal of Industrial Relations* 17, 2, September 1975(b), pp. 225–239. Table on p. 227, provides the data for 1911 to 1971. Further discussion is provided in Margaret Power 'The Making Of A Woman's Occupation' *Hecate* 1, July 1975(a), pp. 25–34. For industrial segregation see Hazel Moir and Joy Selby-Smith, 'Industrial Segregation in the Australian Labour Market' *Journal of Industrial Relations* 21, September 1979, pp. 281–91.

7 Unemployment

1 For discussion of discouraged workers see W. J. Merrilees 'Married Women In The Labour Force: A Note On Discouraged Workers' *Australian Economic Papers* December 1979, pp. 365–7.

2 Data from *Women at Work: Facts and Figures* The Women's Bureau, Department of Employment Education and Training, Canberra, October 1987.

3 Early unemployment figures for women were further distorted by married women being excluded from claiming benefits. See John Steinke, 'Measurement of Unemployment in Australia' *Journal of Industrial Relations* 20, 2, pp. 140–62, June 1978.

4 An interesting sideline to this discussion is the exclusion of housewives from the denominator when calculating female unemployment rates. See Janet L. Johnson 'Sex Differentials In Unemployment: A Case For No Concern' *Journal of Political Economy* 91, 2, 1983, pp. 293–303. For support of this view see Barbara Bergmann 'The Economic Risks Of Being A Housewife' *American*

Economic Review 71, 3, May 1981, pp. 81–5, Bergmann concludes that being a housewife is being a member of the largest single occupation in America.

5 This effect is discussed in Roger J. Bowden 'A Dynamic Model of Cyclical Labour Force Participation' *Economic Record* 56, 155, 1980, pp. 362–73.

6 It is of interest to note this when reading articles such as B. D. Haig and M. P. Wood 'A Simulation Study of Married Women In The Australian Work Force 1961–72' *Australian Economic Papers* December 1976, pp. 171–85. The inference is also obvious in Beth Niemi, 'The Female-Male Differential In Employment Rates' *Industrial and Labour Relations Review* 27, 3, April 1974, pp. 331–50. Niemi concludes that females suffer less unemployment during recessions because they are concentrated in the service industries.

7 Data for Figure 7.1 taken from ABS *Labour Statistics 1982, No 6101* 1983, p. 39. And from ABS No 6203, August 1987.

8 Data from The Department of Education Youth and Training *School Leavers. Eighth Edition, 1987*. Canberra: AGPS, 1987.

9 Data for Table 7.1 comes from ABS, No 6203 *op. cit.*

10 See Moir and Selby–Smith, 1979. This definition was fully discussed with Table 3.3 in Chapter 3.

11 Data for Table 7.2 was taken from ABS No 6203 August 1987.

8 Orthodox theories

1 Gary Becker 'Human Capital' reprinted in Ray Marshall and Richard Perlman *An Anthology of Labor Economics: Reading and Commentary* New York, London, Sydney and Toronto: John Wiley and Sons Inc., 1972, pp. 777–84

2 John T. Addison and W. Stanley Siebert *The Market for Labor: An Analytical Treatment* California: Good Year Publishing Company 1979, pp. 115–19

3 The Human Capital model can be expressed in a simple mathematical form. For example:

$$R = \Sigma(Y_t - X_t) \hspace{3em} \text{eqn 8.1}$$

The return, R, from an extra year of schooling is the sum of the differences between Y_t, the value of expected future earnings, and X_t, the loss incurred in present earnings over the working lifetime, t.

Discounting to give the present value of the extra life time income stream, PR:

$$PR = (Y_t - X_t)(1 + i)^{-t} \hspace{3em} \text{eqn 8.2}$$

Where i is the interest rate at which the individual can borrow funds, or alternatively, the rate that could be obtained by placing those funds in a similarly risky business. Obviously, the shorter the expected working life, t, the higher this rate of return must be in order to make investments in schooling worthwhile.

4 Isabel V. Sawhill 'Economic Perspectives on the Family' re-

printed in Alice H. Amsden, *The Economics of Women and Work* Harmondsworth, Middlesex: Penguin Books Ltd, 1980.

5 For a fuller discussion of the implications of this assumption see C. E. Ferguson, *Microeconomic Theory* 3rd edn. USA: Richard D. Irwin Inc. 1972, pp. 393–426.

6 Gary Becker *A Treatise on the Family* London: Cambridge University Press, 1981. For discussion of inter-generational transmission of advantage see p. 150. For an opposing view see Michael T. Hannan 'Families, Markets and Social Structures' *Journal of Economic Literature* 20, March 1982, pp. 65–72. Hannan criticises Becker for assuming equal, optimal, income levels for all households and for ignoring social and cultural factors.

7 Jacob Mincer 'Labor Force Participation of Married Women: A Study of Labor Supply' reprinted in Amsden *op. cit.* pp. 41–52.

8 This point is debatable, authors such as Barbara Bergmann, 'The Economic Risks of Being a House Wife' *American Economic Review* 71, 2, May 1981, pp. 81–5. Bergmann argues that being a housewife can lower family valuation of that member as well as being a disinvestment in market productivity.

9 Becker *op. cit.* pp. 14–21. For further discussion see Michael R. Ransom 'An Empirical Model of Discrete and Continuous Choice in Family Labour Supply' *The Review of Economics and Statistics* 119, 3, August 1987, pp. 465–72.

10 Mincer's (1980) model of labour supply was given as:

$$M = B_p . Y + YW + u \qquad \textbf{eqn 8.3}$$

Where: M = the quantity of labour supplied to the market

Y = the potential permanent level of family income in wage terms, computed at zero levels of home production and leisure

W = the individual's, with non-market comparative advantage, full time market wage ie their earning power in the market.

u = other factors or tastes

$$Y = X_p + W \qquad \textbf{eqn 8.4}$$

Where: X_p = other sources of family income; this is predominantly the wage of the individual with the comparative advantage for market work

Therefore: $M = B_p (X_p + W) + YW + u$ **eqn 8.5**

$ = B_p X_p + aW + u$ **eqn 8.6**

Where: $a = B_p + Y$ **eqn 8.7**

 and $B_p < 0, Y > 0$.

The parameter, B_p, represents the movement in the labour market involvement of the individual with a comparative advantage in non-market work when the permanent income of the household varies (given that this variation has not been caused by 'a', the non-market specialist's own wage). In other words, B_p

measures the movement in the hours spent in the labour market by the wife when the husband's wage changes, or when they inherit money, etc. The hourly wage rate of the wife is itself held constant when considering B_p. B_p thus symbolises the familiar income effect. Similarly, Y represents the effect of the non-market worker's market earning power when holding the family's income constant. Hence, Y can be considered as the substitution effect; the attractive power of the wage rate in pulling non-market workers into the labour market. Equation 8.7 can be considered as a form of the Slutsky equation (Gravelle and Rees, 1986; 101–103).

11 Mincer provides empirical evidence to support this claim in his article with Polachek, 'Family Investments in Human Capital: Earnings of Women' *Journal of Political Economy* 82, 2, March/April 1974, pp. S77–S110.

12 This is fully pointed out by Ben Porath Yoram, 'Economics and the Family. Match or Mismatch' *Journal of Economic Literature* 20, May 1982, pp. 52–64.

13 Gary Becker 'A Theory of the Allocation of Time' *Economic Journal* 80, September 1965, pp. 493–517. Becker discusses intra family allocations and response to income changes in pp. 512–17.

14 For discussion of the empirical difficulties when attempting to estimate Becker's model see Peter Kooreman and Arie Kapteyn 'A Disaggregated Analysis of the Allocation of Time within the Household' *Journal of Political Economy* 95, 2, 1987, pp. 223–49.

15 Gary Becker *The Economics of Discrimination* 2nd edn, Chicago: Chicago University Press, 1957, p. 59.

16 This is the assumption of utility maximisation.

17 Kenneth Arrow 'Models of Job Discrimination' in A. H. Pascal (ed.) *Racial Discrimination in Economic Life*. Lexington: Lexington Books, 1972.

18 As cited by Paul Milgrom and Sharon Oster 'Job Discrimination, Market Forces and the Invisibility Hypothesis' *Quarterly Journal of Economics* 102, 3, August 1987, pp. 453–76.

19 G. J. Stigler 'The Economics of Information' *Journal of Political Economy* 70, 1962, pp. 94–105.

20 Robert S. Chirinko 'An Empirical Investigation of the Returns to Job Search' *American Economic Review* 72, 3, June 1982, pp. 498–501.

21 For formal statements of the search theory see Tony Lancaster 'Econometric Methods for the Duration of Unemployment', *Econometrica* 47, 1979, pp 939–56. Lancaster constructs a model based on data collected from interviews with a sample of unskilled British workers. And Martin L. Weitzmann 'Optimal Search for the Best Alternatives' *Econometrica* 47, 3, May 1979, pp. 641–55. Weitzmann presents a formal theoretical expression of the search theory.

22 Edmund S. Phelps 'The Statistical Theory of Racism and Sexism' *American Economic Review* 72, 3, June 1982 pp. 498–501.

Consider the following equations:

$$Y_i = Q_i + u_i \qquad \text{eqn 8.8}$$

Where: Y_i = the overall ability test of each applicant
Q_i = the applicants degree of promise or qualification (scaled)
u_i = the error term
i = the pool of job applicants

If the employer has no other information about the job applicant except for Q_i, then, Q_i may be used as a least squares predictor of the applicant's overall ability, Y_i, according to a regression type relation:

$$Q'_i = a'_i.Y_i + u_i \qquad \text{eqn 8.9}$$

$$0 < a_i = \frac{\text{var } Q'_i}{\text{var } Q'_i + \text{var } u_i} < 1. \; E(u_i) = 0.$$

Q_i and Y_i are both deviations from their respective population means and a_i is the probability limit, as N approaches infinity, of the regression coefficient.

When the employer uses sex as a proxy;
$$Q_i = a + X_i + n_i \qquad \text{eqn 8.10}$$

Where: $X_i = (-B + E_i)C_i,$ \qquad eqn 8.11
$B > 0.$
$C_i = 1$ if applicants are female, 0 if male.
X_i = the contribution of social factors believed to be sex related according to equation 8.11.

E_i and n_i are both random variables, normally and independently distributed, with zero mean.

If $H_i = n_i + C_iE_i$ and $Z_i = -BC_i$

therefore:

$$Q_i = a + Z_i + H_i$$
$$Y_i = Q_i + u_i = a + Z_i + H_i + u_i \qquad \text{eqn 8.12}$$

Hence, as Phelps (1982) points out, the test datum can be used in relation with the sex factor to predict the degree of qualification, net of the sex factor, the latter being separately calculable:

$$Q'_i - Z'_i = a_i (Y'_i - Z'_i) + u_i \qquad \text{eqn 8.13}$$

$$0 < a_i = \frac{\text{var } H_i}{\text{var } H_i + \text{var } u_i} < 1$$

or equivalently;

$$Q'_i = \frac{\text{var } H_i}{\text{var } H_i + \text{var } u_i}.Y'_i + \frac{\text{var } u_i}{\text{var } H_i + \text{var } u_i}.Z'_i + u_i. \qquad \text{eqn 8.14}$$

Here it can be seen that the weights (which are applied to the ability test information and the gender orientated information) are inversely related to the variance of the respective disturbance terms corresponding to them. Hence, if growing up female is expected to have disadvantages of the type that will cause inferior work patterns, then $Z_i < 0$ and the employer will expect that the Q_i for women will be less than the Q_i for men, when all other test scores are equal. When there is no differential variability in promise between men and women then var H_i = var n_i and the coefficients in equation 8.14 are independent of C_i.

23 For a more detailed analysis and representation of screening methods see Shiro Yabushita 'Theory of Screening and the Behavior of the Firm: Comment' *American Economic Review* 73, 1, March 1983, pp. 242–5. Yabushita points out that the existence of equilibria in screening models depends upon the assumed behaviour of the firm, rather than on the screening processes.

24 Being 'economically rational' does not lower the costs of discrimination to those affected by these actions. The analyst should be doubly wary of the claim that discrimination is economically rational since the underlying assumption of a group's behavior often goes unproven.

25 For discussion of the adjustments needed when comparing quit rates see Bruce J. Chapman and Heather Prior 'Sex Differences in Labour Turnover in the Australian Public Service' *The Economic Record* 62, 179, December 1986, pp. 496–505

26 If employers do not face full competition it may actually be in their interests to offer lower wages to a group such as females.

9 Institutional theories

1 For a comparison of orthodox models with institutional models see Clair Brown 'An Institutional Model of Wives' Work Decisions' *Industrial Relations* 24, 4, Spring 1985, pp. 183–204.

2 As cited in Peter B. Doeringer 'Determinants of the Structure of Industrial Type Labour Markets' *Industrial and Labor Relations Review* 20, 2, January 1967, pp. 206–20.

3 *ibid.*

4 Michael Piore 'Labor Market Segmentation; To What Paradigm Does It Belong?' *American Economic Review* 73, 3, May 1983, pp. 249–53. See also Doeringer *op. cit.*

5 This point will be returned to in the conclusion of this chapter of the text.

6 See Addison and Siebert *op. cit.* p. 189, for discussion.

7 Paul Osterman 'Employment Structures Within Firms' *British Journal of Industrial Relations* 1981, pp. 349–61.

8 See the introduction to this chapter of the text.

9 It may be in the interest of employers to develop secondary job tasks within their firms and place (*hide*) females in these occupations. 'Then, at a competitive labor market equilibrium, firms profit by hiding talented disadvantaged workers in low-level jobs. Consequently, those workers are paid less on average and promoted less often than others with the same education and ability'.

Paul Migrom, and Sharon Oster 'Job Discrimination, Market Forces, and the Invisibility Hypothesis'. *The Quarterly Journal of Economics*, Vol. 102, Issue 3, August 1987, pp. 453–476.

10 Osterman, 1981.

11 Bernard Elbaum 'The Internalization of Labor Markets Causes and Consequences' *American Economic Review* 73, 2, May 1983, pp. 260–5. And Masanori Hashimoto 'Firm Specific Human Capital As A Shared Investment' *American Economic Review* 71, 3, June 1981, pp. 475–81.

12 For full discussion of labour as a fixed factor see W. Y. Oi, 'Labor as a Quasi-Fixed Factor' *Journal of Political Economy* 70, 1962, pp. 538–55.

13 Typically presented by Becker, see in particular his article, 'Investment in Human Capital: A Theoretical Analysis' *Journal of Political Economy* 70, October 1962, pp. 9–49 (especially 10–15).

14 Monopsonistic competition (Mansfield, 1979; 396–410 and Addison and Siebert, 1979; 46–52) occurs when there are many buyers of a heterogeneous supply of inputs, with some buyers preferring some seller's inputs to other seller's inputs. Therefore, the situation can arise where inputs (workers) rely on a single, or very few, buyers for employment. This employer will face an upward sloping market supply curve for the input. The slope of the curve implies that the price the firm must pay the input will increase with the quantity of the input employed or, in other words, that the marginal expenditure for the input will exceed the input price paid to the last increment of input employed. As a profit maximiser, the firm will employ units of input until the marginal revenue product generated by the input is equal to the marginal expenditure incurred by the firm for the employment of the input. The monopsonist's employment decision, when compared to that of a firm operating in a perfectly competitive market, will be to employ lower levels of the input and to pay this input a lower price.

If women did face a monopsonistic employer, equal pay legislation would, by setting a uniform price for the input employed, cause the firm's marginal expenditure for the input to drop to the level set by the legislated wage rate. Without product market power, the monopsonist's marginal expenditure product will be equal to the value of marginal product, set by a firm operating in competitive input and product markets, which is equal to the wage rate. Hence, equal pay legislation would inspire monopsonist employers to increase both the employment levels and the wage rate of women towards competitive levels.

Thurow extends the model of monopsony power in a logically consistent and valuable manner. He presents an analysis of discrimination in terms of supply and demand elasticities. This analysis has an extra twist because Thurow considers the gains and losses to male employees of employers discriminating against women.

Thurow points out that discrimination is analytically very similar to a uniform drop in the demand curve of the group being discriminated against (Chiplin and Sloane, 1974; 371–402). The vertical distance of the fall in demand representing the size of the discrimination coefficient. The extent of the effect of this employer discrimination on the female work force will, of course, depend on the supply elasticity of female labour and on the male demand elasticity for female labour. In general, the more inelastic the female supply curve the greater the gain from discrimination for the employer. Male employees can gain part of this exploited value via collusion with employers or because the drop in female employment has led to an increase in demand for men. When the elasticity of the female supply curve is zero, male losses from the discrimination against women will be zero. When the elasticity of the female supply curve is infinite, male gains will be zero since the female wage will already be pushed down to its lowest level (equal to their marginal revenue product). However, normally expectations would be that male losses do not exceed male gains unless both the elasticities of supply and demand are large. Hence, it will generally be in the interest of male employees to encourage employers to discriminate against women.

Thurow's model is very difficult to prove empirically, although its theoretical implications are very significant and can lead to conclusions which can be tested empirically.

15 Joan Robinson *Collected Economic Papers* Oxford: Basil Blackwell Publishers, 1973. Robinson discusses the exploitation practiced by those with market power. For an alternative view see M. Brofenbrenner 'Potential Monopsony in Labor Markets' *Industrial and Labor Relations Review* 1, 1956, pp. 577–88. Brofenbrenner concludes that firms will not make the most of their monopsonistic power but will rather offer higher wages to attract high quality workers.

16 The overcrowding model provides an interesting combination of the concepts provided earlier. The origins of the model are usually attributed to Edgeworth (F. J. Edgeworth 'Equal Pay to Men and Women for Equal Work' *Economic Journal* 31, 1922). This model takes as its starting point the possibility of male trade unions being largely responsible for crowding women into comparatively few occupations and that this overcrowding was the main reason for low female wages. Bergmann (Barbara Bergmann 'Occupation Segregation, Wages and Profits When Employers Discriminate by Race or Sex' *Eastern Economic Journal* 1, 2–3, April–July 1974 pp. 103–10) combines Edgeworth's early concept of overcrowding with the differential approach of Becker to consider the link between wage and occupational differences between groups of workers, the following analysis is taken from her 1974 paper.

Consider two occupations, the marginal productivity of a worker in each will be a linear function of the total number of employees in that occupation. It is assumed that the firm is profit maximising and operating in a competitive market. Employers therefore, equate the marginal productivity of workers to the wage rate offered. When an occupation is overcrowded then, by definition, the marginal productivity of each worker will be less than that in an uncrowded occupation. Thus, the overcrowded worker's wage rate will be lower.

If employers distinguish between two categories of employees, say men and women, by believing a crucial difference in productivity exists between the workers of dm in a menial occupation, and dp in a prestige occupation (where dp generally exceeds dm and both can be measured in absolute dollar terms). Then if the female wage is dp dollars less than the male wage in the prestige occupation and dm dollars less in the menial occupation, employers would be indifferent between the two groups in either occupations. However, men would be expected to seek and occupy those relatively scarce jobs in the prestige occupation where their wage rate is the highest. Similarly, the majority of women would be expected to seek employment in the occupation where their wage rate is the highest; in the menial occupation where they will be crowded in with those few men who missed out on the prestige jobs.

In order for there to be no worker migration between the two occupations, dm < [(prestige marginal productivity)—(menial marginal productivity)] < dp, or in algorithm form:

$$\underbrace{\overset{\substack{\text{men in p} \\ \text{and m} \\ \text{women in p}}}{\underset{dm}{}} \quad \overset{\substack{\text{perfect} \\ \text{segregation}}}{\underset{dp}{}} \quad \overset{\substack{\text{men in p women} \\ \text{in p and m}}}{}}_{} \text{MPp–MPm}$$

The crucial difference measure can be considered as a discrimination measurement or coefficient, in which case the overcrowding analysis takes on a slightly different complexity. Now, due to employer discrimination, workers may be placed in sparse or overcrowded occupations which will subsequently alter their marginal productivities bringing them into line with the wages set by the employers. As has already been seen, such behaviour will lower female wages but will raise male wages, the overall effect on the firm's profits of such discrimination is not immediately obvious.

Employer discrimination in competitive market circumstances has always been considered as economically irrational by the orthodox models. The discriminator is not employing solely on efficiency (marginal productivity) grounds, but, is instead letting personal dislikes interfere with profit maximising measures. In contrast, Bergmann's model suggests that systematic occupational segregation by employers represents a form of discrimination which may be profit maximising.

Once again consider two occupations, employees in each are paid according to their marginal productivities. Profits (P) will depend on the production function (f) and its partial derivatives (f1 and f2) and on the distribution of the fixed labour force between the two occupations (L1 and L2).

$$P = f(L1,L2) - L1f1\ (L1,L2) - L2f2(L1,L2) \qquad \textbf{eqn 9.1}$$
remembering $dL1/dL2 = -1$

Then a first order condition for profit maximising will occur when:

$$dP/dL1 = -L1(f11 - f12) - L2(f21 - f22) = 0 \qquad \textbf{eqn 9.2}$$

Since marginal productivities do not appear in this equation, it is not necessary that the marginal productivity of labour be equal in both the occupations. In fact, only when the production function is homogeneous to any degree will profit maximising and equality of the marginal productivities of the two types of labour be consistent with each other, this will not be the general case (Bergmann, 1974; pp. 106–8 also considers the case of monopsonistic employers where discrimination may be profit maximising given the constraints Thurow discusses).

Bergmann's conclusion is of obvious theoretical interest, it has now been shown to be profit maximising for an employer without individual market power to discriminate via occupational segregation.

17 See Bergmann, 1974 p. 279.
18 Barbara Bergmann 'Curing High Unemployment Rates Among Women' reprinted in Amsden, 1980, pp. 350–58.
19 Francine Blau *Equal Pay in the Office* Lexington: Lexington Books, 1977. In particular see the first 20 pages.
20 The employer does not set the wage rate for workers. Rather, the employers choose the type of workers which will be offered the high paying jobs and those that will be offered the low paying jobs.
21 As was found in 'Human capital', Chapter 8.

10   Radical theories

1 It is no longer assumed that employers are competitive and workers are paid according to how productive they are, as stated in the orthodox and institutional models discussed in Chapters 8 and 9. The Marxian framework provides a totally different explanation of the labour market.
2 Michael Reich, David M. Gordon and Richard C. Edwards 'A Theory of Labor Market Segmentation' *American Economic Review* 63, 2, May 1973, pp. 359–65. Also David M. Gordon, Richard C. Edwards and Michael Reich *Segmented Work, Divided Workers; The Historical Transformation of Labor in the United States* London, New York and Sydney: Cambridge University Press, 1982.
3 The first epoch, from the 1820s until the 1890s, covers the initial stages of industrialism and is characterised by 'competitive capitalism' as worker competed against worker and capitalist against capitalist. During this period, it is argued that automation and

the factory system began to replace previously skilled craft occupations with specialised unskilled work tasks. The dispossessed craftsmen and peasant farmers migrated to the large manufacturing towns seeking work and wages, only to find large scale unemployment and poverty. Those lucky enough to find work would not necessarily escape the poverty as the army of desperate unemployed constantly competed for jobs and effectively bid the wage rate down to a mere subsistence level. The hardships of the working class were heightened by the cyclical swings in production. The capitalists faced major imperfections in information concerning the demand for their goods, especially overseas demand. Believing there to be great demand they would swing into full capacity production, only to find that the demand had already been sated, forcing them to close their factories until inventories ran down again. When the factories closed the working class were left with no means of support and very little hope of receiving aid from the State (since new Poor Laws were deliberately drafted to discourage the poor seeking such assistance). The workers responded to their increasing suffering with political uprisings and militancy, threatening the capitalists' hold on the means of production. In turn, the capitalists responded by devising a new form of labour market organisation and transforming the society into the second stage of capital accumulation, the period of homogenisation.

During this second stage of capital accumulation the process of deskilling and automating work tasks rapidly accelerated. Managers adopted Taylorism and 'scientific' work ordering techniques as they actively sought to standardise work conditions and homogenise the labour force. The working class began to consist of large masses of semi to unskilled workers sharing very similar work experiences and often living in large communities in housing provided by their employer. Hence, their everyday lifestyles were almost identical.

These workers developed strong social support groups and would no longer compete against each other to undercut wage or working conditions. They recognised themselves as having the same basic interests. As the epoch entered its decay process, with the associated cyclical swings in business activity, the workers realised that their interests were in conflict with those of their employers. They joined together in large unions, such as the Industrial Workers of the World (IWW), and carried out very successful and powerful campaigns which were increasingly targeted at the class structure and the social system itself.

As competition had decreased between the workers during the period of homogenisation, it also decreased amongst the capitalists, leading to a concentration of market power in the hands of a few large monopolistic firms. When the homogenisation period culminated in the great depression these powerful captains of industry took control. They transformed the social system to provide their huge firms with stable markets, thereby creating the third stage of capital accumulation, the period of segmentation running from the 1930s onwards.

4   M. Reich, D. M. Gordon and R. C. Edwards, 1973 pp. 361–2

5   These stratified control systems aimed at removing the worker's focus from the capitalist, redirecting their dissatisfaction toward the worker's immediate supervisor, who was usually also a member of the working class. Simultaneously, the internal structure offered bribes for worker acceptance in the form of guaranteed promotion to the supervisor's position with its higher wage rate and artificially created social status.

6   Horizontal movements across these job ladders are exceptionally difficult, not because of low productivity or lack of training but rather, because of the physical or social characteristics of the individual which had originally excluded them at the port of entry to that job ladder.

7   Thus, if males are striking for higher wages employers may pay high wages to females to carry out the work of the males and thereby break the strike. Often, just the threat of bringing in migrant or female replacements will prevent the strike from occurring.

8   As discussed in 'Intra-Firm Segmentation' in Chapter 9.

9   The large monopolist companies use the secondary sector for irregular sub-contracting jobs, and for further segmenting the labour market.

10   The evolution of technology is also claimed to have aided the process of segmentation. Technology has typically been developed within and for the primary sector increasing the separation between the primary and secondary sectors. Technology has also increased the artificial separation of primary workers by each working with a slightly different machine. Also, since technology is often of a similar form to earlier technological advances, it has been easier for firms to retrain those employees already slightly familiar with a particular machine. This enables the firm to claim some justification, on productivity grounds, for maintaining their original employees. However, this does not provide any justification for their original arbitrary segmentation and training of workers.

The authors are somewhat weak on the issue of the evolution of technology. Segmentationists argue that the labour organisation of each period reflects the power relationships and the state of struggle between the workers and the capitalists of the previous period. Thus when capitalists devise a new institutional framework, within which the process of capital accumulation takes place, they will explicitly consider the current nature and extent of labour power and the limitations with the previous form of labour organisation which enabled this power to arise. The new period will be structured so as to avoid this form of labour power being sustained or redeveloped. This weakness is apparent in Gordon, Reich and Edwards 1973. Furthermore this difficulty does not seem to have been corrected in the 'second generation' of

Segmentationist theorists either, see Michael Reich 'Segmented Labour Markets; Time Series Hypothesis and Evidence *Cambridge Journal of Economics* 8, 1984, pp. 63–81.
11 Reich, 1984, pp. 65–6.
12 This can be easily discovered by a quick survey of the volumes of *Radical American*.
13 This distinction between the Segmentationist and the Neo-Marxists may appear to be somewhat arbitrary, and the two do have definite similarities, however, they also have dissimilarities. The point is that neo-Marxists see the capitalist period as essentially a *single* epoch which is progressing in a continuous pre-determined manner due to the evolution of technology and the dialectic. The segmentationists describe *three* intermittent stages which are characterised by the independent actions of the capitalist class.
14 Jane Humphries 'Class Struggle and the Persistence of the Working Class Family' *Cambridge Journal of Economics* 1, September 1977, pp. 241–58.
    Humphries argues that Marx and Engels perceived the family as merely an outgrowth of property relations and that, since the proletariat would own no property, there was no reason for the family structure to survive among the working class. In fact, as early as 1845, Marx claimed that among the proletariat the family had already been abolished. Humphries highlights two issues (which are essential to the study of women in both market and non-market work) that Marx abstracted from in analysing the role of the working class family. First, she argues that Marx ignored the *use* value of commodities produced by the non-market labour of household members. The domestic labourer produces a surplus of goods and services beyond those needed for their own subsistence. The immediate beneficiaries of this surplus value are the other members of the family whose standard of living will subsequently be higher. Since these goods and services are not sold in the market place they do not have a monetary value, instead they have a *use* value for the family. For Marx, the only use values produced are within the capitalist sector. Indeed, under capitalism the division of labour is extremely marked, since domestic labour is separated from the prevalent means of production and from market exchange relations. Since household workers are not paid a wage for their work it is often rendered invisible and seemingly valueless. However, domestic labour will, nevertheless, create use value and increase the family's standard of living and should therefore be considered in the analysis of the family's welfare.
    Second, Marx introduced, but did not develop, the argument that the male wage (which was set at a level required to provide sustenance for the male worker and his dependent family) could be broken down into a smaller sum if the capitalist could force those women and children to work for their own keep. The capitalist could thereby capture the surplus value of such family

members' non-market work and significantly lower the family's standard of living. Marx described this action by the capitalists as universal proletarianisation. The natural development of attempted universal proletarianisation is a battle by the working class to maintain the 'family wage' and the family structure, enabling wives' and children's non-market work to raise the family's standard of living. Humphries implies that capitalists have found it more politically stable not to force universal proletarianisation upon the working class.

15 Humphries encounters ambiguity over this point; on the one hand, she acknowledges that males (both labourers and capitalists) recognise that female labour can generate surplus value which males want to conquer. On the other hand, however, she discusses the servile role played by housewives and that publicity opposing female market labour involvement has reinforced the male attitude that females have inferior productivity.

16 Marxist models typically fail to consider the individual's effect on society, just as the neo-Classical models typically fail to consider the society's effect on the individual. See Michael J. Piore, 1983 pp. 252–3.

17 Joan W. Scott and Louise A. Tilly, 'Women's Work and the Nineteenth Century Europe'. Reprinted in Amsden, 1980 pp. 91–125.

18 Scott and Tilly, 1980 p. 119.

19 Scott and Tilly argue that industrialisation led to a breakdown of strong family ties as traditional families, operating on long held values, sent their daughters to urban regions to work in the new mills or as domestic staff and return their earnings to their parents. However, the relatively high wages the siblings received reversed the traditional dependency role of children and parents, creating tension. This effect was magnified by the long distances and high immigration rates which cut children off from their parents' influence, instead children were more greatly influenced by their peers. These siblings increasingly considered their jobs as avenues of social and occupational mobility rather than temporary earnings to aid the family. So, the mutual support system between children and parents broke down to become a one-sided aid system, whereby parents supported children until the children were old enough to leave home and support themselves.

20 Michael Crozier *The World of the Office Worker* Chicago: University of Chicago Press, 1971. Especially pages 16–19, see also Bravermann, 1974 pp. 348–9.

21 Jill Rubery 'Structured Labour Markets, Worker Organization and Low Pay' *Cambridge Journal of Economics* 2, 1, March 1978, pp. 17–36.

22 Rubery provides interesting criticisms of many of the other models we have discussed. She rejects the 'low level equilibrium trap' theories presented by the orthodox analysts in their discussions of non-competing groups within the market. In particular, Rubery criticises the off-handed attitude these orthodox analysts maintain on discrimination. She argues that, orthodox authors explain

away the origins of inequality as being created outside of the market system, and that the market is therefore not responsible for discrimination. However, they simultaneously use the presence of discrimination within the society as a device which creates barriers to perfect market operations. The resultant distorted market operations reinforce the original inequality and discrimination within the society. Hence, even after acknowledging the effect discrimination can have on equality via the market system, orthodox authors claim that, since the origins of discrimination are exogenous to the market, discrimination can be justifiably ignored. Rubery's model explicitly includes discrimination as an endogenous factor thereby allowing the analyst to directly focus on this problem, its causes and cures.

Rubery also rejects the explanation for dual market structures provided by Doeringer and Piore, who claim that the role of technology or divergent industrial development can explain the labour market structure. She bases her rejection on two main criticisms. First, the dualist model incorrectly claims that internal market structures developed in response to an increase in job specific skills when, in fact, work has become increasingly deskilled. And second, the dualist model ignores the power of both capitalists and workers to establish market structures that have only limited relation to the presiding state of technology.

Finally, Rubery rejects the radical approach of the Segmentationists whereby the origins of stratification in the labour force are entirely based on the capitalists' needs to divide and rule the labour force. Within the segmentation model the capitalist class explicitly considers the dominant form of labour power at the time of transformation and the weaknesses in the earlier market structure that enabled this power to arise. The capitalists will then devise a new market structure that can suppress this worker power. Rubery wants to explicitly consider the power of workers in the present period to force capitalists to structure the labour market in a way that partly satisfies the workers. She claims that the radicals' emphasis on class action ignores the actions of individuals, firms and unions, who may often find that their own self interested actions clash with their general class's interests.

In summation, the problems with the present labour market models are due to their concentration, almost exclusively, on the actions and economic motivations of the employers and the capitalists at the expense of the effective power of worker organisation (Rubery, 1978 *op. cit.* p. 20).

23 Repeated here from the earlier section for the reader's ease. She separates the capitalist period into two phases. In the first phase industrialists sought to replace the general skills of the craftsman/peasant farmer with job specific skills more suitable for the specialised work in industry. In the second phase capitalists used technology and scientific management to conscientiously deskill workers, removing all traces of mental labour from their work and creating a constantly increasing proportion of alienating

occupations. Each new phase of capitalist expansion displaces labour from production outside the capitalist mode and creates new supplies of labour for these inferior occupations. Thus, as capitalism expanded into domestic production, females were released on to the labour market and took up employment in these alienating work tasks. See also 'Neo-Marxists' earlier for discussion of Humphries' views.

24   Carol O'Donnell, *The Basis of the Bargain: A Study of the Sexual Division of Labour in Four Areas of Work in NSW 1950–1981.* Unpublished thesis submitted for a PhD, Macquarie University, 1982. Especially pp. 81–101. Or, for a more concise discussion see Carol O'Donnell 'Market Theories of the Labour Market and Women's Place Within It' *Journal of Industrial Relations* 26, June 1984, pp. 147–65 (Especially pp. 160–65).

11   Legislation and affirmative action

1   The Human Rights Commission in collaboration with the Office of the Status of Women and the Attorney General's Department *A Guide to the Commonwealth Sex Discrimination Legislation* AGPS Canberra: March 1984.

2   Ms O'Neil was the first Sex Discrimination Commissioner. She was appointed in July 1984. See 'Sex Discrimination Commissioner Appointed' *Human Rights: Newsletter of the Human Rights Commission* 10, Australia, July 1984, p. 1.

3   Australia ratified this United Nations Convention in 1983.

4   See National Committee on Discrimination in Employment and Occupation *Tenth Annual Report, 1982–83* AGPS Canberra: pp. 31–45.

5   P. A. Riach and J. Rich 'Testing for Sexual Discrimination in the Labour Market' *Mimeo, Monash University* November 1987. Forthcoming in *Australian Economic Papers*, December 1987.

6   *ibid.* p. 15.

7   Margaret Thornton 'Job Segregation, Industrialization and the Non-Discrimination Principle' *Journal of Industrial Relations* 25, March 1983, pp. 38–50.

8   Bruce J. Chapman 'Labour Turnover and Wage Determination' *Australian Economic Papers* 26, 48, June 1987. Amongst Chapman's findings is that the wage received is linked to the expected *ex ante* quit rates rather than the quit rates actually revealed by the worker (*ex post*).

9   For discussion see Andrew Byrne 'The Sex Discrimination Act 1984. The First Three Years' *Current Affairs* 64, 4, September 1987, pp. 12–19.

10   This point is discussed by Glenda Strachan 'Equal Employment Opportunity and Industrial Relations: The Path to Equality' *Journal of Industrial Relations* 29, 2, June 1987, pp. 190–206.

11   Department of Prime Minister and Cabinet *Affirmative Action For Women* 1 and 2, AGPS Canberra: May 1984.

12   Vol 1, Affirmative Action for Women, 1984 *op. cit.*, p. 8. See also

Department of Prime Minister and Cabinet *Affirmative Action Implementation Manual* AGPS Canberra: 1984.

13 Australian Federal Parliament *Affirmative Action (Equal Employment Opportunity for Women) Act 1986* No. 91 of 1986. 14525/86. Cat. No. 86 5024 4.

14 See subsection 7(b), (ii) and (iii), Affirmative Action Bill, 1986 *op. cit.*, pp. 5–6.

15 For discussion see Affirmative Action Agency *Affirmative Action: Guidelines for Implementation in Institutions of Higher Education* AGPS, Canberra: March 1987.

16 Where an objective is defined as a 'qualitative measure or aim, expressed as a general principle, designed to achieve equality of opportunity for women in employment matters, being a measure that can reasonably be implemented by the relevant employer within a specified time'. See section 8, subsection 3, Affirmative Action Bill 1986 *op. cit.*, page 7.

17 A forward estimate differs in definition from an objective only in that a forward estimate '*may* be expressed in numerical terms' (our emphasis). Section 8, subsection 3, Affirmative Action Bill 1986 *op. cit.*, page 7.

18 A guide to this statistical breakdown is provided in *Affirmative Action Implementation Manual* (Second Edition), Canberra: AGPS February 1986, pp. 14–30.

19 Although some authors claim that goals and quotas can become effectively the same thing. For instance Gabriel Moens makes the interesting claim that 'both a goal and a quota require the selection and the appointment of applicants less qualified than others who, under traditional meritocratic selection criteria, would have been appointed'. However, we have not found that employment opportunities always go to the most qualified. Rather it was found in Chapter 3 that the qualifications of females are under-utilised by employers. Quote taken from Gabriel Moens 'Affirmative Action: The New Discrimination' *Centre for Independent Studies Policy Monographs 8* NSW: The Centre for Independent Studies Ltd, December 1985, p. 27.

20 As cited in Richard Blandy and Judith Sloan 'The Australian Labour Market' *Australian Bulletin of Labour* 12, 2, March 1986, p. 89.

21 It may be argued that the Affirmative Action Bill will be less effective by not stipulating that females be given preference.

> *I will argue that women are often not perceived to be as highly qualified as they really are. Thus, when the qualifications of candidates are compared, a woman may not be thought equally (or more highly) qualified, even when she is. Affirmative action programs which require hiring of equally qualified women will therefore be ineffective.*

See Laura M. Purdy 'In Defence Of Hiring Apparently Less Qualified Women' *Journal of Social Philosophy* 15, 2, pp. 26–33, Summer 1984, quote taken from p. 26. Purdy claims that employers downgrade the performance of females' academic work, creating a situation where females acquire poorer standard qualifications than males due to discrimination. An interesting argument concerning affirmative action is also presented in Sandra G. Harding 'Is the Equality of Opportunity Principle Democratic?' *The Philosophical Forum* 10, 2–4, pp. 206–223, Winter-Summer 1978–79. For a consideration of the effectiveness of American affirmative action programs see Andrea H. Beller 'The Impact Of Equal Opportunity Policy On Sex Differentials In Earnings And Occupations' *American Economic Review* 72, 2, pp. 171–5, May 1982.

22   See Glenn C. Loury 'Economics of Affirmative Action: Is Equal Opportunity Enough?' *American Economic Review* 71, 3, pp. 122–26, June 1981. Further discussion is provided in Gayle Binion 'Affirmative Action Reconsidered: Justifications, Objections, Myths and Misconceptions' *Women & Politics* 1, 1, Spring 1987, pp. 43–62. Gale S. Baker 'Is Equality Enough?' *Hypatia* 2, 1, Winter 1987, pp. 63–65.

See also Purdy, 1984; Loury, 1981; Beller, 1982; Harding, 1978; Lundberg and Startz, 1983 (especially p. 345); Larwood, Gutek and Gattuker, 1984. All of these articles have substantial bibliographies with further references for the interested reader.

23   Quote from Loury, 1981, p. 122.

24   Sharon Simon 'The Survival of Affirmative Action in the 1980s' *Labor Studies Journal* 10, 3, Winter 1986, pp. 261–280, p. 261.

25   '...already participants can point to achievements and they feel that the final three months will demonstrate even further progress'. Affirmative Action Resource Unit *Affirmative Action for Women: A Progress Report on the Pilot Program* Office of the Status of Women, Department of Prime Minister and Cabinet, Canberra: AGPS May 1985, p. 31.

26   Bruce J. Chapman 'Affirmative Action For Women: Economic Issues' Centre For Economic Policy Research, *Australian National University Discussion Paper* 97, June 1984.

27   For discussion of statistical discrimination and the need for affirmative action see Shelley J. Lundberg and Richard Startz 'Private Discrimination and Social Intervention in Competitive Labor Markets' *American Economic Review* 73, 3, pp. 340–47, June 1983.

12   Conclusion

1   It was the strong impression of this study that the influence of groups within the labour market (where groups are organisations larger than individuals and smaller than classes) provided much of the explanation for the position of women in the labour force, as well as the structure and development of the labour market. Examples of these groups are women, trade unions, employers, men, professional bodies, racial or religious groups, etc. The two major theories that supported the models presented here cannot explain the presence of groups.

Orthodox economic theory assumes that workers in the labour market are self interested *individuals* who will compete against each other to maximise their own interests. The radical theory assumes that all workers are members of a single *class*, the proletariat, and that the members have common interests and common goals.

The models presented in Chapters 8 and 10 are based on either one of these two theories and yet many of the models have made assumptions that blatantly contradict the assumptions of the theory that is supporting their model.

When authors construct models that discuss pressures across groups, they implicitly assume that the inclusion of small group power will not affect the operations of the economy in totality. They continue to rely on either the radical or orthodox economic frameworks to explain all those facets of the economy that they have not discussed in their model. However, the labour market appears to be made up of very large and powerful groups. These groups may have a very substantial effect on the labour market and the labour market may, in turn, have a very substantial effect on the economy. The predictions of contemporary models are based on their analysis of group pressures. However, the very formation and sustained existence of these groups contradict the underlying theories that the models use. The authors step away from their supporting theories when making their assumptions about group behaviour. Yet, they rely on the supporting theory to explain many of the remaining assumptions that they are making. This contradiction appears to be creating many of the difficulties the models faced. There would seem to be much need for labour market analysts to seriously consider the inferences of the paradigms they adopt. There also appears to be a great need for a new theory which can consistently consider the overlap between the individual and their social setting.

2 Market power can be removed by removing the source of this power. This may involve selling large firms and distribution of shares amongst many owners or removing government protection in the forms of tariffs, patents, sole production rights, etc.

Bibliography

Addison, John T. and Siebert, W. Stanley *The Market for Labor: An Analytical Treatment* California, Good Year Publishing Company 1979

Australian Federal Parliament *Affirmative Action (Equal Employment Opportunity for Women) Act 1986* No 91 of 1986. 14525/86 Cat. No 86 5024 4

Affirmative Action Resource Unit 'Strategies for Employers for Supporting Female Apprentices in Non-Traditional Trades' *Affirmative Action Issues Paper No 1* Canberra: Department of Prime Minister and Cabinet, Office of the Status of Women, January 1985

—— *Affirmative Action For Women: A Progress Report on the Pilot Program* Canberra: Department of Prime Minister and Cabinet, Office of the Status of Women, May 1985

Affirmative Action Agency *Affirmative Action: Guidelines for Implementation in Institutions of Higher Education* Canberra: AGPS, March 1987

Amsden, Alice H. *The Economics of Women and Work* Harmondsworth, Middlesex: Penguin Books Ltd, 1980

Anderson, Michael and Ross, Brent 'Labour Force Projections and Tables of Working Life: A Preliminary Investigation' *Paper Presented to the 16th Conference of Economists* Surfers Paradise, August 1987

Australian Public Service *Statistical Year Book, 1985–86* Canberra: AGPS, 1986

Bain, George Sayers and Price, Robert 'Who is a White Collar Employee?' *British Journal of Industrial Relations* 10, 3, 1972, pp. 325–39

Baker, Gale S. 'Is Equality Enough?' *Hypatia* 2, 1, Winter, 1987, pp. 63–65

Baldwin, Sue, and Walpole, Francis *Women, Affirmative Action and Democracy* Canberra: Department of Employment and Industrial Relations. Working Environment Branch. AGPS, 1986

Becker, Gary *The Economics of Discrimination* 2nd edn, Chicago: Chicago University Press

—— 'Investment in Human Capital: A Theoretical Analysis' *Journal of Political Economy* 70, October 1962, pp. 9–49

—— 'A Theory of the Allocation of Time' *Economic Journal* 80, September 1965, pp. 493–517

—— 'Human Capital' reprinted in Ray Marshall and Richard Perlman *An Anthology of Labor Economics: Reading and Commentary* N.Y., London, Sydney, Toronto: John Wiley and Sons Inc., 1972 pp. 777–84

—— *A Treatise on the Family* London: Cambridge University Press, 1981

Behrmann, J. R., Sickles, Robin C. and Taubman, Paul 'The Impact of Minimum Wages on the Distribution of Earnings for Major Race Sex Groups: A Dynamic Analysis' *American Economic Review* 73, 4 September 1983, pp. 766–88

Beller, Andrea H. 'The Impact Of Equal Opportunity Policy On Sex Differentials In Earnings And Occupations' *American Economic Review* 72, 2, May 1982, pp. 171–75

Berger, Suzanne and Piore, Michael, *Dualism and Discontinuity in Industrial Society* New York, Melbourne and Sydney: Cambridge University Press, 1980

Bergmann, Barbara 'The Effect of White Incomes of Discrimination in Employment' *Journal of Political Economy*, 79, 1971

—— 'Occupation Segregation, Wages and Profits When Employers Discriminate by Race or Sex' *Eastern Economic Journal* 1, 2–3, April–July 1974, pp. 103–10

—— 'Curing High Unemployment Rates Among Women', reprinted in Amsden, Alice H. *The Economics of Women and Work*, Harmondsworth Middlesex: Penguin Books Ltd, 1980, pp. 350–58

—— 'The Economic Risks of Being a House Wife' *American Economic Review* 71, 2, pp. 81–85, May 1981

Binion, Gayle 'Affirmative Action Reconsidered: Justifications, Objections, Myths and Misconceptions' *Women and Politics* 7, 1, Spring 1987, pp. 43–62

Blandy, Richard and Sloan, Judith 'The Australian Labour Market March 1986' *Australian Bulletin of Labour* 12, 2, March 1986, pp. 82–90

Blau, Francine *Equal Pay in the Office* Lexington, Massachusetts and Toronto: Lexington Books, 1977

Bowden, Roger J. 'A Dynamic Model of Cyclical Labour Force Participation' *Economic Record* 56, 155, 1980, pp. 362–73

Braverman, Harry *Labour and Monopoly Capital; The Degradation of Work in the Twentieth Century* USA: Monthly Review Press, 1974

Brofenbrenner, M. 'Potential Monopsony in Labor Markets' *Industrial and Labor Relations Review* 9, 1956, pp. 577–88

Brown, Clair, 'An Institutional Model of Wives' Work Decisions' *Industrial Relations* 24, 4, 1985, pp. 182–204

Bureau of Labour Market Research 'Structural Change and the Labour Market' *BLMR Research Report No. 11* Canberra: AGPS 1987

Burton, Clare, with Hag, Raven and Thompson, Gay *Pay Equity and Job Evaluation in Australia* Canberra: AGPS, 1987

Byrnes, Andrew 'The Sex Discrimination Act 1984: The First Three Years' *Current Affairs* 64, 4, September 1987, pp. 12–19

Chapman, Bruce J. 'Affirmative Action For Women: Economic Issues' *Centre For Economic Policy Research ANU Discussion Paper* No 97, June 1984

—— 'Sex Differences in Earnings: Changes over the 1970s in the Australian Public Service', prepared for presentation in B. J. Chapman, J. E. Isaac, and J. R. Niland, (eds), (1984a) *Australian Labour Economics Readings* 3rd edn, Australia: MacMillan Co., of Australia Pty Ltd, 1984b

—— 'Sex and Location Differences in Wages in the Australian Public Service', *Centre for Economic Policy Research, ANU Discussion Paper* No 98, July 1984c/1985. More recently published in *Australian Economic Papers* 24, 45, December 1985, pp. 296–309

—— 'Labour Turnover and Wage Determination' *Australian Economic Papers* 26, 48, June 1987, pp. 119–29

Chapman, Bruce J. and McKeen, Pat 'Absenteeism of South Australian Teachers' Mimeo, Adelaide: Flinders University of South Australia, 1975

Chapman, B. J., Isaac, J. E. and Niland, J. R. (eds) *Australian Labour Economics Readings* 3rd edn, Australia: MacMillan Co. of Australia Pty Ltd, 1984a

Chapman, Bruce J. and Prior, Heather 'Sex Differences in Labour Turnover in the Australian Public Service' *Centre for Economic Policy Research, ANU Discussion Paper* No 118, April 1985/86. More recently published in *The Economic Record* 62, 179, December 1986, pp. 497–504

Chapman, Bruce J. and Mulvey, Charles 'An Analysis of the Origins of Sex Differences in Australian Wages' *Journal of Industrial Relations* 28, 4, December 1986, pp. 504–21

Chiplin, Brian and Sloane, Peter J. 'Sexual Discrimination in the Labour Market' *British Journal of Industrial Relations* 12, 3, November 1974, pp. 371–402

Chirinko, Robert S. 'An Empirical Investigation of the Returns to Job Search' *American Economic Review* 72, 3, June 1982, pp. 498–501

Cogan, John F. 'Fixed Costs And Labor Supply', *Econometrica* 49, 4, July 1981, pp. 945–62

Crozier, Michael *The World of the Office Worker* Chicago: University of Chicago Press, 1971

Das Gupta, Prithwis 'Comment on Suzanne Bianchi and Nancy Rytina's "The Decline in Occupational Sex Segregation during the 1970's: Census and CPS Comparisons"' *Demography* 24, 2, May 1987, pp. 291–5

Dawkins, Peter and Norris, Keith 'Casual Employment in Australia' *Paper Presented to the 16th Conference of Economists* Surfers Paradise, August, 1987

Department of Employment and Industrial Relations *Women, Affirmative Action and Industrial Democracy* Baldwin, Frances and Walpole, Sue. Working Environment Branch. Canberra: AGPS, Australia 1986

Department of Employment, Education and Training, *School Leavers,*

Eighth Edition, 1987 Research and Statistics Branch. Canberra: AGPS, August 1987

—— *1986 Survey of Sex-Differentiating Provisions in Federal Awards* The Women's Bureau, The Office of the Status of Women. Canberra: AGPS, 1987

—— *Women and Work* The Women's Bureau. The Office of the Status of Women. Canberra: AGPS, April 1987

Department of Prime Minister and Cabinet *Affirmative Action For Women: A Policy Discussion Paper* 1 and 2, Canberra: AGPS, May 1984

—— *Affirmative Action Implementation Manual* Canberra: AGPS, 1984

—— *Affirmatve Action Implementation Manual* 2nd edn, Canberra: AGPS, February, 1986

—— Affirmative Action Resource Unit 'Strategies for Employers for Supporting Female Apprentices in Non-Traditional Trades' *Affirmative Action Issues Paper No 1* Canberra: Office of the Status of Women, January 1985

Doeringer, Peter B. 'Determinants of the Structure of Industrial Type Labour Markets' *Industrial and Labor Relations Review* 20, 2, January 1967, pp. 206–20

Duncan, O. D. and Duncan, B. 'A Methodological Analysis of Segregation Indexes' *American Sociological Review*, 20, April 1955, pp. 210–17

Eccles, Sandra 'The Role of Women in The Australian Labour Market: A Survey of the Literature' *Journal of Industrial Relations* 24, September 1982, pp. 315–36

Edgeworth, F. J. 'Equal Pay to Men and Women for Equal Work', *Economic Journal* 31, 1922

Elbaum, Bernard 'The Internalization of Labor Markets Causes and Consequences' *American Economic Review* 73, 2, May 1983, pp. 260–5.

Engels, F. *The Conditions of the Working Class in England in 1844* London: George Allen and Unwin Ltd, 1968

Ferguson, C. E. *Microeconomic Theory* 3rd edn, USA: Richard D. Irwin Inc., 1972

Gordon, David M., Edwards, Richard C. and Reich, Michael *Segmented Work, Divided Workers; The Historical Transformation of Labor in the United States* London, NY, and Sydney: Cambridge University Press, 1982

Gravelle, H. and Rees, R. *Microeconomics* NY: Longman Group Ltd, 1986

Gregory, R. G. and Duncan, R. C. 'Segmented Labour Market Theories and the Australian Experience of Equal Pay for Women' *Journal of Post Keynesian Economics* 3, 3, Spring 1981, pp. 403–29

Griffin, Gerard 'Personal Characteristics and Industrial Militancy in White Collar Unions' *Journal of Industrial Relations* 23, June 1981, pp. 274–81

Groshen, Erica L. 'The Structure of the Female/Male Wage Differential: Is It Who You Are, What You Do, or Where You Work?' *Federal*

Reserve Bank of Cleveland Working Paper No. 8708 Cleveland, USA, September 1987

Haber, Sheldon E., Larnas, Enrique J. and Green, Gordon, 'A New Method of Estimating Job Separations by Sex and Race' *Monthly Labour Review* June 1983, pp. 20–7

Haig, B. D. 'Sex Discrimination in the Reward for Skills and Experience in the Australian Labour Force' *Economic Record* 58, 160, March 1982, pp. 1–10

Haig, B. D. and Wood, M. P. 'A Simulation Study of Married Women In The Australian Work Force 1961–72' *Australian Economic Papers* December 1976, pp. 171–85

Hannan, Michael T. 'Families, Markets and Social Structures' *Journal of Economic Literature* 20, March 1982, pp. 65–72

Harding, Sandra G. 'Is The Equality of Opportunity Principle Democratic' *The Philosophical Forum* 10, 2–4, Winter–Summer 1978–79 pp. 206–23

Hashimoto, Masanori 'Firm Specific Human Capital As A Shared Investment' *American Economic Review* 71, 3, June 1981, pp. 475–81

Hoss, Ida Russakoff 'The Impact of Office Automation on Office Workers', *International Labour Review* 80, October 1960

Human Rights Commission, in collaboration with the Office of the Status of Women and the Attorney General's Department, *A Guide to the Commonwealth Sex Discrimination Legislation* Canberra: AGPS, March 1984

—— 'Sex Discrimination Commissioner Appointed' *Human Rights: Newsletter of the Human Rights Commission* 10, July 1984a p. 1

Humphries, Jane, 'Class Struggle and the Persistence of the Working Class Family' *Cambridge Journal of Economics* 1, September 1977, pp. 241–58

Johnson, Janet L. 'Sex Differentials In Unemployment: A Case For No Concern' *Journal of Political Economy* 91, 2, 1983, pp. 293–303

Karmel, T. and Maclachlan, M. 'Sex Segregation Increasing or Decreasing?' *Paper Presented to the 16th Conference of Economists* Surfers Paradise, August 1987

Kenyon, Peter and Dawkins, Peter, 'Explaining Labour Absence in Australia' *Murdoch University Economics Programme Working Papers, Paper No 1* Western Australia, August 1987

Kelley, Maryellan R. 'Discrimination in Seniority Systems: A Case Study' *Industrial And Labor Relations Review* 36, 1, October 1982, pp. 40–5.

Kooreman, Peter and Kapteyn, Arie 'A Disaggregated Analysis of the Allocation of Time Within the Household' *Journal of Political Economy* 95, 2, 1987, pp. 223–49

Kramar, Robin 'Affirmative Action: A Challenge to Australian Employers and Trade Unions' *Journal of Industrial Relations* 29, 2, June 1987, pp. 169–89

Lancaster, Tony, 'Econometric Methods for the Duration of Unemployment' *Econometrica* 47, 1979, pp. 939–56

Lansbury, Russell, 'The Growth and Unionization of White Collar

Workers in Australia: Some Recent Trends' *Journal of Industrial Relations* 19, March 1977, pp. 34–49

Larwood, Laurie, Gutek, Barbara and Gattiker, Urs E. 'Perspectives on Institutional Discrimination and Resistance to Change' *Group and Organization Studies* 9, 3, September 1984, pp. 333–52

Leigh, J. Paul 'Sexual Differences in Absenteeism' *Industrial Relations* 22, 3, Fall 1983, pp. 349–61

Lewis, Donald E. 'Comparative Quit Rates of Men and Women' *Journal of Industrial Relations* 21, September 1979, pp. 331–50

—— 'The Measurement of the Occupational and Industrial Segregation of Women' *Journal of Industrial Relations* 24, September 1982, pp. 406–23

—— 'The Measurement and Interpretation of the Segregation of Women in the Workplace' *Journal of Industrial Relations* 25, September 1983, pp. 347–52

Lewis, Donald E. and Shorten, Brett 'Female Participation in the Australian Labour Force' *Australian Bulletin of Labour* 13, 4, September 1987, pp. 237–63

Lewis, H. G. *Unionism and Relative Wages in the United States: An Empirical Study* Chicago: The University Of Chicago Press, 1963

Linneman, Peter 'The Economic Impacts of Minimum Wage Laws: A New Look At An Old Question' *Journal of Political Economy* 90, 3, 1982, pp. 443–69

Loury, Glenn C. 'Economics of Affirmative Action: Is Equal Opportunity Enough?' *American Economic Review* 71, 3, June 1981, pp. 122–6

Lundberg, Shelley J. and Startz, Richard 'Private Discrimination and Social Intervention in Competitive Labor Markets' *American Economic Review* 73, 3, June 1983, pp. 340–7

Mansfield, Edwin *Micro Economics* 3rd edn, USA: W.W. Norton and Co. Inc., 1979

McGavin, P. A. 'Equal Pay for Women: A Reassessment of the Australian Experience' *Australian Economic Papers* 22, June 1983, pp. 48–59

—— 'Equal Pay for Women: A Postscript' *Australian Economic Papers* 22, June, 1983a, pp. 65–7

—— 'The Measurement of Occupational and Industrial Segregation of Women: A Re-appraisal' *Journal of Industrial Relations* 24, 1983b, pp. 339–45

Merrilees, W. J. 'Married Women In The Labour Force: A Note On Discouraged Workers' *Australian Economic Papers* December 1979, pp. 365–7

Meyer, Peter J. 'Segmented Work, Divided Workers' *Journal of Economic Literature* 21, September 1983, pp. 1038–9

Meyer, R. H. and Wise, D. A. 'Discontinuous Distributions' *Econometrica* 51, 6, November 1983a, pp. 1677–98

Milgrom, Paul and Oster, Sharon 'Job Discrimination, Market Forces, and the Invisibility Hypothesis' *The Quarterly Journal of Economics* 102, 3, August 1987, pp. 453–76

Mincer, Jacob 'Labor Force Participation of Married Women: A Study of Labor Supply'. Reprinted in Amsden, Alice H. *The Economics of*

Women and Work Harmondsworth Middlesex: Penguin Books Ltd, 1980.

Mincer, Jacob and Polachek, S. 'Family Investments in Human Capital: Earnings of Women' *Journal of Political Economy* 82, 2, March/April 1974, pp. S77–S110

Moens, Gabriel 'Affirmative Action: The New Discrimination' *Centre for Independent Studies Policy Monographs No. 8* The Centre for Independent Studies, New South Wales, December, 1985

→ Moir, Hazel and Selby-Smith, Joy 'Industrial Segregation in the Australian Labour Market' *Journal of Industrial Relations* 21, September 1979, pp. 281–91

Morrison, Phillip and Morrison, Emily, *Charles Babbage and His Calculating Machines; Selected Writings By Charles Babbage and Others* New York: Dover Publications Inc., 1961

Nakamura, Alice and Nakamura, Masao 'A Comparison Of The Labor Force Behaviour Of Married Women In The United States And Canada, With Special Attention To The Impact Of Income Taxes' *Econometrica* 49, 2, March 1981, pp. 451–84

National Committee on Discrimination in Employment and Occupation *Tenth Annual Report, 1982–83*, Canberra: AGPS, 1983

Nicholson, Nigel, Brown, Colin A. and Chadwick-Jones, J. K. 'Absence from Work and Job Satisfaction' *Journal of Applied Psychology* 61, 6, 1976, pp. 728–37

Niemi, Beth, 'The Female–Male Differential In Employment Rates' *Industrial and Labour Relations Review* 27, 3, April 1974, pp. 331–50

O'Donnell, Carol, *The Basis of the Bargain: A Study of the Sexual Division of Labour in Four Areas of Work in NSW 1950–1981* Unpublished thesis submitted for a PhD, Macquarie University, 1982

—— 'Market Theories of the Labour Market and Women's Place Within It' *Journal of Industrial Relations* 26, June 1984, pp. 147–65

—— *Getting Equal: Labour Market Regulation and Women's Work* Sydney: Allen and Unwin 1988

Oi, W. Y. 'Labor as a Quasi–Fixed Factor' *Journal of Political Economy* 70, 1962, pp. 538–55.

—— 'Neglected Women and Other Implications of Comparable Worth' *Contemporary Policy Issues* 4, 2, 1986, pp. 21–32

Olson, Craig A. and Becker, Brian E. 'Sex Discrimination in the Promotion Process' *Industrial and Labor Relations Review* 36, 4, July 1983, pp. 624–41

O'Neill, June 'A Time Series of Women's Labor Force Participation' *American Economic Review* 71, 2, May 1981, pp. 76–80

Osterman, Paul 'Employment Structures Within Firms' *British Journal of Industrial Relations* 1981, pp. 349–61

Paringer, Lynn 'Women and Absenteeism: Health or Economics' *American Economic Review* 73, 2, May 1983, pp. 123–38

Phelps, Edmund S. 'The Statistical Theory of Racism and Sexism' *American Economic Review* 72, 3, June 1982, pp. 498–501

Piore, Michael 'Labor Market Segmentation; To What Paradigm Does It Belong?' *American Economic Review* 73, 3, May 1983, pp. 249–53

Power, Margaret 'The Making Of A Woman's Occupation', *Hecate* 1, July 1975, pp. 25–34

—— 'Women's Work Is Never Done By Men: A Socio-Economic Model Of Sex Typing In Occupations' *Journal of Industrial Relations* 17, 2, September 1975a, pp. 225–239.

Powles, Margaret *Women's Participation in Tertiary Education: A Review of Recent Australian Research* Commonwealth Tertiary Education Commission, Belconnen, ACT, 1986

Purdy, Laura M. 'In Defence Of Hiring Apparently Less Qualified Women' *Journal of Social Philosophy* 15, 2, Summer 1984, pp. 26–33

Quinlan, Daniel C. and Shackelford, Jean A. 'Labour Force Participation Rates of Women and the Rise of the Two Earner Family' *American Economic Review* 70, 2, May 1980, pp. 209–13

Ransom, Michael R. 'An Empirical Model of Discrete and Continuous Choice in Family Labour Supply' *The Review of Economics and Statistics* 69, 3, August 1987, pp. 465–72

Reich, Michael 'Segmented Labour Markets; Time Series Hypothesis and Evidence' *Cambridge Journal of Economics* 8, 1984, pp. 63–81

Reich, Michael, Gordon, David M. and Edwards, Richard C. 'A Theory of Labor Market Segmentation' *American Economic Review* 63, 2, May 1973, pp. 359–65

Riach, P. A. and Rich, J. 'Testing for Sexual Discrimination in the Labour Market' *Mimeo Monash University*. Forthcoming in *Australian Economic Papers*, December, 1987

Robinson, Joan *Collected Economic Papers* Oxford: Basil Blackwell Publishers, 1973

Rubery, Jill 'Structured Labour Markets, Worker Organization and Low Pay' *Cambridge Journal of Economics* 2, 1, March 1978, pp. 17–36

Sawhill, Isabel V. 'Economic Perspectives on the Family' reprinted in Amsden, Alice H. *The Economics of Women and Work*, Harmondsworth Middlesex: Penguin Books Ltd, 1980, pp. 125–40

Scott, Joan W. and Tilly, Louise A. 'Women's Work and the Nineteenth Century Europe' reprinted in Amsden, Alice H. *The Economics of Women and Work* Harmondsworth Middlesex: Penguin Books Ltd 1980, pp. 91–125

Short, Christine 'Equal Pay – What Happened?' *Journal of Industrial Relations* 28, 3, September 1986, pp. 315–35

Simon, Sharon 'The Survival of Affirmative Action in the 1980s' *Labor Studies Journal* 10, 3, Winter 1986, pp. 261–80

Sorensen, Elaine 'Effects of Comparable Worth Policies on Earnings' *Industrial Relations* 26, 3, Fall 1987, pp. 227–39

Steers, R. and Rhodes, Susan R. 'Major Influences on Employee Attendance: A Process Model' *Journal of Applied Psychology* 63, 4, 1978, pp. 391–401

Steinke, John 'Measurement of Unemployment in Australia', *Journal of Industrial Relations* 20, 2, June 1978, pp. 140–62

Stigler, G. J. 'The Economics of Information' *Journal of Political Economy* 70, 1962, pp. 94–105

Strachan, Glenda 'Equal Employment Opportunity and Industrial Relations: The Path to Equality' *Journal of Industrial Relations* 29, 2, June 1987, pp. 190–296

Thornton, Margaret 'Job Segregation, Industrialization and the Non-Discrimination Principle', *Journal of Industrial Relations*, 25, March 1983, pp. 38–50

Weitzmann, Martin L. 'Optimal Search for the Best Alternatives' *Econometrica* 47, 3, May 1979, pp. 641–55

Women's Bureau *Women at Work: Facts and Figures* The Office of the Status of Women Department of Employment Education and Training. Canberra, Australia. October, 1987

—— *1986 Survey of Sex-Differentiating Provisions in Federal Awards* The Office of the Status of Women. The Department of Employment, Education and Training, Canberra: AGPS, 1987

—— *Women and Work* The Office of the Status of Women, The Department of Employment, Education and Training, Canberra: AGPS, April 1987

Yabushita, Shiro 'Theory of Screening and the Behavior of the Firm: Comment', *American Economic Review* 73, 1, March 1983, pp. 242–5

Yoram, Ben Porath, 'Economics and the Family. Match or Mismatch' *Journal of Economic Literature* 20, May 1982, pp. 52–64

Australian Bureau of Statistics (ABS)

ABS *Cross Classified Characteristics of Persons and Dwellings: 1981 Census of Population and Housing, Australia, No. 2452.0* Canberra: AGPS, October 1983

—— *Australian Health Survey 1977–78, No 4311*, Canberra: AGPS, 1979

—— *Australian Health Survey 1983, No 4311*, Canberra: AGPS, 1986

—— *Australian Health Survey 1977–78: Days of Reduced Activity Due to Illness or Injury, No 4321*, Canberra: AGPS, 1981

—— *Labour Statistics Australia, 1982, No 6101* Canberra: AGPS, 1983, 1986, 1987

—— *The Labour Force, Australia, No 6203* Canberra: AGPS, May 1984, May and August 1987

—— *Labour Force Experience, No 6206* Canberra: AGPS, February 1983

—— *Labour Mobility, No 6209* Canberra: AGPS, February 1983 and February 1986

—— *Labour Force Status and Educational Attainment, No 6235* Canberra: AGPS February 1983 and February 1986

—— *Earnings and Hours of Employees, No 6304* Canberra: AGPS, August 1984

—— *Weekly Earnings of Employees (Distribution), No 6310* Canberra: AGPS, May 1983

—— *Award Rates Of Pay Indexes, No 6312* Canberra: AGPS, June 1984

—— *Trade Union Statistics, No 6323* Canberra: AGPS, April 1984, May 1986 and 1987

Index